The B Ging

A Memoir of Family, War
and Resilience

Ging Dormido

with Ron Dormido

Copyright © 2025 Ging Dormido and Ron Dormido

All rights reserved.

ISBN: 9798303655065

This book is a memoir, presenting the author's recollections and interpretations of past experiences. It is not intended to serve as a strictly factual account. To protect the privacy of individuals, some names and identifying details have been changed. Additionally, certain events have been condensed, combined, or restructured for narrative coherence, and some dialogue has been recreated to enhance storytelling.

Dedication

To God Almighty, for His boundless grace and unwavering love that has sustained me throughout my life.

To my beloved children, grandchildren, and great-grandchildren, my heart's greatest joy and the true treasures of my life.

Preface

It was a scene that played out at pretty much most social gatherings when I was a kid. Lots of delicious Filipino food. Men drinking and playing cards in one area. Some women indulging in their vice as well, gossiping above the sounds of clicking white mahjong tiles. The rest of the grownups talking story in the living room.

My Mom was usually at the center of the latter group, telling tales about the time she won the Miss 7-Up competition in Cebu, or that she was a black market vendor during the War, or how she was always picked to be the queen of some fiesta because she was the pretty mestiza girl. I had heard them all before, as had most of my cousins.

We'd take a momentary break from playing tag, hide and seek, or some other outdoor activity to grab a snack, usually lumpia. We made a beeline for the food table. Scooped up the goods with our grubby hands, hoping no one would make us wash up first.

"What's your Mom talking about now?" asked a cousin.

I shrugged my shoulders, half a lumpia already in my mouth, happily crunching away. He shrugged his shoulders in turn, and with lumpia in hand we were off again.

Fast forward to adulthood. Social gatherings were still pretty much the same: drinking, gambling, talking story. The older grownups are a little more gray, a little more wrinkled, and a little more rotund. Now my kids and my nieces and nephews are the ones playing outside. I'm on the periphery of the story telling, but close to the food table. A prime spot.

Seems like the grandchildren have grown accustomed to hearing Grandma's stories too.

My niece and nephew come in from outside, making a beeline for the food table—specifically the lumpia.

They notice Grandma and her seemingly captivated audience.

"Hey Uncle, what's Grandma talking about now?"

Munching on a lumpia, I shrug my shoulders.

My niece shrugs her shoulders in response. The two cousins grab a fistful of lumpia and off they go.

"Hey, make sure you wash your hands first!" I call out.

Sometimes I would tease my Mom about her storytelling, but only at gatherings of immediate family.

"We all had to do our part to support the family during the war. It was a matter of survival. That's how I got started with the black marketing."

"Mom, did that really happen?" I would ask, in a playful, sarcastic voice.

"Of course it did, why would I lie?" And then she would playfully swat me on the arm with her large print edition Reader's Digest.

About a year before the COVID-19 pandemic, I stopped by to visit my Mom and found her at her dining table (which also serves as her work desk, sewing table, and so on) leafing through a blue, hard cover binder.

"What are you looking at Mom?"

"Remember Jan? My neighbor here at the condo, the one who passed away a few years ago? She always said that I had the most interesting life. And she started writing my memoirs but unfortunately she never finished. I was hoping someone could help me with it."

I started leafing through the binder. Maybe a dozen or so nicely formatted, laser printed pages. The stories were all familiar; I had heard them many times before. This was the first time seeing them in print.

"I think I could help out with this in my spare time, Mom."

She closed the binder and handed it to me.

"Perfect! When will it be finished?"

I started to backtrack a little.

"Well, Mom I always have so much going on at work, but I'm sure I can find time to work on it."

She looked a bit skeptical.

"Okay, make sure to keep me updated on it."

In the fall of 2019 I decided to take a sabbatical. Work had become stressful and I was feeling burnt out. Some time off would do me good, I thought.

Perfect timing. A few months later the whole world was on lockdown. My Mom wasn't driving anymore and with me not working, it was easier to spend time with her and help out with things.

"How are you coming along with my memoirs?"

I didn't know how to tell her that I hadn't opened that binder since she gave it to me a few years back.

"Oh, it's coming along okay I guess."

A little white lie.

"When do you think it'll be finished?"

"I'm not sure. You know, Mom, unfortunately Jan didn't write down a lot of your other stories so we'll probably need more material."

"Okay, well I can tell you my other stories and you can write them down."

She was determined. I wasn't working now, so I couldn't really procrastinate on this project anymore.

"That's a good idea. Might be good if I recorded our interviews. I can work with the transcripts from the interviews."

And so it began. Over the next several months, I recorded interviews with my mom. Channeling my inner journalist, I relied on simple, yet probing, questions to draw out details and piece together a coherent chronology. It wasn't always easy. My mom's stories often unfolded in a non-linear fashion, veering off into tangents or losing focus. Still, I gently guided her back on track whenever needed.

The interview sessions quickly became something she looked forward to. She seemed more energized and animated during our conversations, whether we conducted them in person, over Skype, or by telephone. Mom always enjoyed telling stories about her life, but this time there was a greater sense of purpose.

I found myself cherishing these sessions as much as she did. While many of the stories were familiar, I discovered new layers of detail I'd previously overlooked. Occasionally I learned about events I had been completely unaware of.

Gradually, these stories took on a deeper significance for me. I could vividly visualize the events she described, like scenes from a movie playing in my mind. My mom's recollections resonated with me in a way they never had before. I began to see them not just as her experiences, but as moments that had profoundly shaped my own life. The events of her past were not just chapters in her personal story; they were the foundation of our family's shared history. These retellings captured pivotal moments, some of which influenced my journey as deeply as they had shaped hers.

As you read through this book, you may come across unfamiliar locales or phrases. But the underlying themes will surely be familiar: tales of love, happiness, sorrow, and sacrifice. Themes that have served as the basis for storytelling for centuries. Themes that are universal in everyone's journey through life. My sincere hope is that you, the reader, will see this collection of stories as more than a chronicle of an individual's life story. I hope that you will see them as an homage to the stories that were once taken for granted, and now, through the lens of personal growth and life's challenges, are embraced with a newfound understanding and appreciation.

Ron Dormido
October 2025

Acknowledgments

This book would not have been possible without the unwavering support of my family and friends. While there are too many to name individually, I extend my heartfelt thanks to each of you for your love, encouragement, and belief in me, especially during moments when I doubted myself. Your support gave me the strength to keep going.

To my son, Ron, I owe my deepest gratitude. You have been far more than a co-author; you have been my confidant, sounding board, and tireless advocate. Your dedication to this project has been extraordinary. From recording countless interviews to meticulously researching dates, places, and events, your attention to detail brought this story to life. This book is as much a testament to your efforts as it is to the journey it captures. Thank you for everything.

CONTENTS

Dedication	i
Preface	iii
Acknowledgments	ix
1 In The Beginning	1
2 Weekend Freedom	4
3 Lice And Borrowed Earrings	7
4 Breakfast With A Lizard	11
5 Tabi Po And Other Superstitions	13
6 Leaving Cebu	16
7 Manila Bound	21
8 New Life In Manila	23
9 Dinalupihan	27
10 Mama Doray's Vices	34
11 Sunday Mornings In Old Manila	38
12 First Communion	43
13 Meaning Of War	46
14 Arrival	48
15 Illusion Of Normalcy	50
16 Losses Of War	54
17 Zonas	57
18 Seeing Dead People	63
19 Matinee At The Ideal	68
20 Weight Of Hunger	75
21 Lola Sima	79
22 Turning Tide	85
23 "V" For Victory	88
24 A GI's Warning	92
25 An Unexpected Visitor	97
26 Cebu Bound	104

27 Homecoming	108
28 Inez	111
29 Discomforts Of Home	118
30 The Long Walk	122
31 Sweet Taste Of Rebellion	125
32 Noli Me Tángere	129
33 Movie Night	135
34 Glimpse Into The Unknown	140
35 New Beginnings	144
36 Dance Hall Days	149
37 Orlando	152
38 The Signs	156
39 City Lights	160
40 Random Caller	165
41 Love And Porridge	171
42 The Promise	175
43 Crossroad	179
44 A Bright Future	186
Epilogue	191
A Life Lived	193
What's In A Name?	217
About The Authors	219

1 In The Beginning

I was placed with another family when I was just a baby. At first glance, it might seem unthinkable for parents to part with their infant daughter. But this was not an act of abandonment. What began as a temporary arrangement turned into years of separation that lasted throughout the war. This decision set me on a path far different from the one my parents might have envisioned. The story of my life unfolds as a tale of two families—my biological and my adoptive—but before delving into that, let me start at the beginning.

I was born on November 23, 1931, on the island of Cebu in the Philippines. At the time, my family lived in the Sikatuna Extension neighborhood in Cebu City. I was the fifth child of Caridad Garcia Estrella and Jose Ramon Moro. My father, Peping (pronounced PEH-PING), graduated with a degree in chemistry from Silliman University. He worked as a pharmaceutical salesman before venturing into entrepreneurship, eventually establishing several pharmacies. My mother, Caridad (Caring, pronounced KAH-REENG), was a dedicated housewife who expertly managed the household and family.

With four older siblings, my mother had her hands full. Thankfully, she had domestic staff to assist with childcare, cooking, and housekeeping. Life in our home, though modest, was stable and secure.

In those days, it wasn't uncommon for parents to have one of their children raised by another family, often due to financial constraints. Stories of such arrangements persist even today. However, that wasn't the case with my parents. While they were not wealthy, they had the means to raise me alongside my siblings. So why, then, did they entrust me to another family?

The answer lies in the teenage girl next door, who fell in love with the newborn baby of the Ramon family.

Our neighbors in Sikatuna Extension were the Peñafiel family. Emilio (Papa Emilio) and Teodora Peñafiel had four children: Carlota, Jose (Joseling), Maria Luisa (Nena), and Rosario (Tito). Papa Emilio was a graduate of Ateneo de Manila, a prestigious Jesuit university renowned for producing prominent Filipino figures, including José Rizal, the national hero of the Philippines.

With a degree in accounting, Papa Emilio was an intelligent and resourceful man. Originally from Manila, the Peñafiels had moved to Cebu a few years before I was born so that he could establish a hardware store. Teodora (Mama Doray, pronounced DOH-RYE) was a housewife whose child-rearing responsibilities had already diminished by the time they relocated, as her children were mostly grown.

The youngest Peñafiel child, Tito, was a teenager of 15 or 16 when I was born. As the story goes, Tito was immediately captivated by the newest member of the Ramon family—me. She visited daily, carrying me around and tending to me as though I were her own. Even with the help of domestic staff, my mother managed a busy household; Tito's attention must have been a welcome relief.

Tito would often take me to her home next door and care for me there. During my first year, while I was still nursing, Tito would bring me back to my mother for feedings, then immediately return me to the Peñafiel household. Before long, I was spending so much time with them that they began to see me as part of their family.

As a toddler, I spent most of my time with the Peñafiels, often staying overnight in a room they had prepared just for me. Their house eventually became my second home. As Tito approached high school graduation, her focus shifted to her future—education and work—and her mother, Mama Doray, took on a more significant role in caring for me.

By the time I turned four, my biological family had grown with the birth of my brother Nene, followed about a year later by another brother Benjie. By the time I was four, I was practically a full-fledged member of the Peñafiel household. I grew deeply attached to the Peñafiels, particularly to Mama Doray and Papa Emilio. With their own children nearly independent, my presence seemed to rekindle their parental instincts and fill the void of an impending empty nest.

As the "baby" of their household, I was doted on and spoiled like an only child. There, I was the center of attention, whereas at home, I had to share my parents' focus with my siblings. During those formative years, the bond between me and my adoptive family deepened to the point that I often preferred being with the Peñafiels over my own family.

When I was about five years old, the Peñafiels announced they were moving to Logarta Street, another part of Cebu. They asked my parents if they could take me with them. My mother was reluctant, but she faced pressure from my father and my grandmother, Lola Julia. For Mama Caring, it was an agonizing decision to give up what was essentially primary custody of her child to another family, even if they would only be a few miles away.

Ultimately, my parents agreed. Mama Doray and Papa Emilio assured my mother they would care for me as their own, guarantee my schooling, and bring me to visit on weekends. Bound by those promises, my mother reluctantly allowed me to move with the Peñafiels to their new residence on Logarta Street.

2 Weekend Freedom

While the Peñafiels doted on me and indulged me, Mama Doray maintained a strict approach to raising me. I followed a regimented schedule that included going to school, completing household chores, and attending church every Sunday. My daily routine left little room for interaction with other children. If there were kids my age in the neighborhood, I have no memory of them because Mama Doray did not allow me to play with them. She once explained that she didn't want me associating with children whose parents she didn't know—and apparently, she didn't know many of the neighborhood families.

The closest thing I had to a friend on Logarta Street was the Peñafiel's domestic helper, Bonifacio. Bonifacio was a teenage boy, around 14 or 15 years old, who assisted with housekeeping tasks, particularly polishing the hardwood floors in the Peñafiel's home. Mama Doray was meticulous about maintaining spotless, highly polished floors. Beyond his duties around the house, Bonifacio also served as my escort to kindergarten.

The Peñafiel's home was less than half a mile from my school, The Little Flower of Jesus. Although it was just a five-minute walk, the trip often took longer because I insisted on riding my tricycle. I had received the tricycle around the time I started school and loved riding it, despite the uneven sidewalks and frequent distractions along the route. Since the tricycle couldn't be left at school, Bonifacio had the added task of carrying it back home after dropping me off and retrieving it again when he came for pickup. Despite the inconvenience, Bonifacio never complained, at least not within earshot.

The lack of companions my age was one of the reasons I eagerly anticipated weekend visits with my mother and siblings at Sikatuna Extension. While I enjoyed being pampered by the Peñafiels and treated like an only child, I longed for the freedom to wander the neighborhood and play with other kids—things I wasn't allowed to do while living with them. At Sikatuna, I could do all these things, and it was exhilarating.

My older brother Julio was a natural leader among the neighborhood kids, and most of them gravitated toward him, following him wherever he went. Julio also had a knack for coming up with creative—and sometimes mischievous—ideas to entertain the group. One of his more ingenious schemes involved charging the neighborhood kids five centavos for the thrill of "riding" a dilapidated old car.

Our house in Sikatuna was built over an open carport, where an ancient, rusted-out car sat. It was little more than a hollow shell—stripped of its parts—but it still had wheels and a steering wheel. The carport's dirt floor sloped downward to an unpaved driveway that led to the street.

Fortunately, a slight depression at the end of the driveway prevented the car from rolling into the street—at least in theory. For many of these children, who had never been inside a real car, the bumpy, brief ride was worth every centavo. However, there was a catch: after every ride, all the kids eager for another turn had to band together and push the heavy car back up the incline. This task, challenging enough for adults, was even more difficult—and risky—for a group of scrawny kids.

Looking back, it's astonishing that none of us were injured or that the car never rolled uncontrollably into the street, causing an accident. As children, we didn't dwell on the dangers. Our determination to enjoy the "ride" kept us going, and we somehow managed to push the car back up the driveway multiple times during my weekend visits. In the process, Julio pocketed several centavos, the kids had their fun, and no one got hurt. All in all, it felt like a win-win situation!

One of Julio's other ideas to entertain us was to put the smaller kids inside a large spinning barrel—a makeshift "ride" we called the "tumble-down." It was located in a field near Zapatera Elementary School, close to where my family lived in Sikatuna. I'm not sure what the barrel's original purpose was, but it was large enough to fit two or three small kids, which made it seem perfect for our "ride"—or so we thought at the time.

We quickly learned that riding in a spinning wooden barrel was far less enjoyable—and much more painful—than we'd imagined. Picture being wedged inside a large, unpadded barrel with one or two other kids, then spun around. At first, the slow, gentle rotations were bearable, even a bit fun. So, we urged the spinner—my brother Julio—to speed things up. But as the barrel gained momentum, the force of it began to slam us against the hard wooden walls and into each other. What started as a fun ride quickly turned into something more like torture. We screamed, "Stop! Stop!" but the spinning only grew faster. Through our cries, we could hear Julio laughing outside the barrel, savoring our desperate pleas and clearly enjoying our discomfort.

Some of our other neighborhood adventures included playing in the shallow river behind Zapatera Elementary. We'd splash around in the cool water to escape the summer heat or search for tadpoles and insect larvae swimming near the surface. Sometimes we'd dig along the muddy banks with sticks, hoping to uncover hidden treasures. These simple pleasures of childhood were the moments I cherished most, and I missed them dearly whenever I returned to the Peñafiel's home.

3 Lice And Borrowed Earrings

Returning to the Peñafiels after weekends with my family was always a source of frustration for Mama Doray. I always came back in a state that could only be described as a disaster. A stickler for cleanliness and hygiene, she insisted I bathe daily while under her care. So, imagine her shock—or perhaps disgust is a more fitting word—when she came to pick me up and found me dirty, disheveled, and with mud from the riverbank caked beneath my fingernails. I looked (and smelled) like a common street urchin! Occasionally, I'd even bring home an unwelcome surprise: lice.

As soon as we got back to Logarta Street, Mama Doray would waste no time beginning her rigorous cleaning and delousing routine. It always started with removing my dirty clothes—often the same ones I had worn since leaving on Friday. Then came a thorough scrub from head to toe, administered by none other than Mama herself, followed by her careful inspection and treatment of my scalp.

Bathing me was one of the ways Mama Doray spoiled me. From the time I was a baby until around the age of nine or ten, she insisted on giving me baths herself. While most kids my age could—and probably should—bathe on their own, hygiene was paramount to her. She didn't trust me not to cut corners, and, truthfully, I didn't mind. There was something comforting about her meticulous care, and I rather enjoyed the attention.

As odd as it may sound, I even liked the process of having my scalp deloused. It felt almost like a head massage. Mama Doray would sit in her chair while I sat or knelt on a cushion at her feet, facing forward so she could comb through my hair. Using a fine-toothed comb, she searched for nits—lice eggs—attached to strands of hair. This part of the process wasn't always pleasant because the fine-toothed comb would sometimes pull my hair. The part I liked came when she found a nit. She'd squeeze it between her thumbnails with a satisfying little pop, her fingers pressing gently against my scalp in the same motion.

Once satisfied that I was properly cleaned and free of lice, she would ready me for bed, tucking me in to prepare for the start of a new week. Yet, she knew this cycle would repeat the following Sunday, when I'd return from my family's home in much the same condition.

Another source of frustration for Mama Doray was the mysterious disappearance of my earrings whenever I visited my family. The earrings were a gift from her—real gold, no less—and I'd often return home without them. The culprit? My older sister Helen, who had a habit of borrowing my jewelry and conveniently forgetting to return it.

Helen, a teenager at the time, was several years older than me. Whenever I visited my family during my kindergarten years, she had a routine question for me. In her playful tone, she would ask, "Ging, are you in school already?"

Eager to share, I would reply in English, "Yes! I go to Little Flower of Jesus! And my teacher is Ms. Banpan!"

Helen loved hearing my excited response. She would giggle every time, later teasing me about how my accent made it sound like I was saying, "I go to Little Plow-wer op Jee-soos!" She found it absolutely adorable and never tired of asking me the same question just to hear me say it again.

In addition to my school updates, Helen also took a liking to my earrings. Mama Doray enjoyed dressing me up in pretty clothes, complete with earrings that matched. She'd had my ears pierced when I was about three or four and gifted me small gold earrings to mark the occasion. She insisted on real gold because, as she explained, my skin was sensitive and couldn't handle anything less.

Helen, ever the fashionable teen, decided those earrings would look great on her, especially when she went out with her friends. "Ging, can I borrow your earrings?" she asked sweetly. Wanting to please my big sister, I happily agreed. Unfortunately, Helen forgot to return them, and being a little kid, I didn't think to ask for them back.

When I returned to the Peñafiels, Mama Doray immediately noticed the absence of my earrings. "Ging, what happened to your earrings?" she asked, her tone both curious and exasperated.

"I let Helen borrow them," I replied innocently.

"Well, you make sure you get them back from Helen," she instructed. I promised I would, but being a little kid, I forgot all about it.

The following week, when I visited my family again, Mama Doray sent me off with another pair of earrings, determined that I should look nice. Helen, of course, noticed the new earrings and, as before, asked if she could borrow them. Wanting to stay on my big sister's good side, I agreed again.

When I returned home to the Peñafiels without the second pair, Mama Doray was incredulous. "Ging, where are your earrings this time?"

"Helen borrowed them," I explained matter-of-factly.

She could hardly believe it. "Again? How could you let her take them and not get them back?"

From that point on, Mama Doray decided it was best if I didn't wear any jewelry when visiting my family. Though she could have spoken to my mother or Helen directly about the missing earrings, she chose not to make an issue of it. Looking back, I imagine she must have been both annoyed and amused by the whole situation—an example of her enduring patience and practicality.

Despite the frustration my home visits must have caused, Mama

Doray never once complained. She understood the importance of spending time with my family and bore the burden of cleaning me up and the loss of the earrings with patience.

4 Breakfast With A Lizard

Just like my family's house on Sikatuna, the Peñafiels' house on Logarta Street was built above an open carport, where Mama Doray ran a *sari-sari* store—a small neighborhood sundry shop. Because she didn't have a permit, Mama Doray was careful to avoid creating a conspicuous storefront. Nevertheless, she managed to attract regular customers and run a moderately successful enterprise.

True to her nature, Mama Doray approached running the sari-sari with diligence and discipline. An early riser, she made sure to start each day with purpose. The shop was always well-stocked with supplies that she purchased at the local market, and sometimes I would accompany her on these trips. At the market, she bought essentials like rice, dried fish, spices, and other household staples. She also received morning deliveries of fresh *pandesal*—soft, slightly sweet bread rolls that are a beloved Philippine staple. The pandesal was particularly popular, with people stopping by to buy a roll or two for breakfast or lunch on their way to work.

Some of my fondest memories are of mornings spent with Mama Doray at a small table in the sari-sari, sharing breakfast. We'd eat fresh pandesal with coffee—though my cup was mostly milk with just a little bit of coffee. For a time, we had an unexpected guest during these morning rituals: a *tuko* lizard. These lizards, named for the distinct "TU-KO, TU-KO" sound they make, are a common sight in the Philippines. This particular lizard would slowly crawl down the wall and approach the breakfast table, seemingly as curious about us as we were about it. Before long, it became bold enough to accept small pieces of pandesal from us. In the Peñafiel household, this little tuko was the closest thing we had to a pet.

One morning, the lizard stopped visiting. Curious, I asked Mama Doray, "Ma, why doesn't the tuko come to visit us anymore?"

She replied gently, "Maybe he moved to another house."

In hindsight, the lizard likely reached the end of its natural life, but Mama Doray chose to spare me from the reality of death, offering an explanation that comforted my young mind. Her answer satisfied me completely, and I never questioned it further.

5 Tabi Po And Other Superstitions

Superstitions and myths have always been woven into Filipino culture, especially during my childhood. It was a simpler time, before televisions became commonplace, and belief in the supernatural ran deep. In the evenings, Mama Doray—and, during visits to my biological family, Mama Caring—would often pass the time recounting stories of mythical creatures believed to dwell among us. These beings lived under dirt mounds or hid among the trees: creatures like the *duwende*, mischievous fairy-like beings, and the *aswang*, terrifying shape-shifting vampires. Alongside these tales, everyday superstitions handed down through generations also shaped our daily routines, sometimes with amusing consequences.

One of my earliest memories of our superstitions is learning the sacred rule of *tabi po*, an expression that loosely translates to 'excuse me' or 'let me pass.' We would say it when walking near trees, rocks, or any place that might be inhabited by spirits or mythical beings. I was only five when I learned to murmur tabi po before running past the mango tree in our yard or any anthills I encountered while playing. I didn't fully understand who or what I was addressing, but I whispered it religiously, terrified that some tiny creature might pinch my toes if I forgot.

When I was about eight, my older brother Julio took every opportunity to tease me about the spirits and creatures our family warned us about. One evening at dusk, as we walked home from a long day exploring a nearby stream, we passed a tall guava tree, heavy with ripe fruit. I tugged at Julio's arm, begging him to stop so I could pick one. With a mischievous grin, he looked up at the fruit dangling from the branches and whispered, 'Are you sure you want one? Those might be the duwende's *itlog* (testicles).' My eyes widened as I imagined a grumpy duwende lurking among the branches, waiting to pounce if I dared touch his "fruit." I was so terrified, I ran all the way home. Breathless and close to tears, I told Mama Caring, who promptly scolded Julio for scaring me. But that didn't stop him or my other siblings from laughing at the fright he'd given me. For years afterward, I eyed any fruit tree with suspicion, still half-believing Julio's tale and giving it a wide berth just in case I disturbed a disgruntled spirit.

Family dinners were often lively and full of surprises, thanks to our superstitions. One dinner in particular comes to mind. I had just dropped my spoon when Mama Doray, without missing a beat, announced, 'A guest is coming!' I didn't understand how a dropped spoon could predict visitors, but as a child, I loved the idea of a surprise guest appearing out of nowhere. Joseling, chuckling, added, 'It will be a woman—a spoon means a woman.' Sure enough, a few hours later, one of Tito's co-workers arrived unannounced. Moments like these only deepened my belief that maybe, just maybe, there was something to these superstitions.

We were also told not to sleep with wet hair to avoid headaches or nightmares. As a child who hated bedtime and loved baths, I found this rule frustrating. One especially warm evening, I took a late bath and was tiptoeing back to my room with my hair still damp when Mama Doray caught me. "*Ay nako* Ging, you'll dream of aswang tonight!" she scolded, wagging her finger in warning. I was skeptical that wet hair could bring anything worse than a damp pillow, but I hardly slept a wink that night. Every rustle outside my window made me flinch, conjuring images of all kinds of scary creatures drawn to my wet hair.

Then there was the practice of not sweeping the floor at night, as it was believed to drive away luck or wealth. This rule was confusing for me, but Mama Doray was strict about it. One evening, I dropped some peanut shells by the dinner table and tried to sweep them up. Her eyes widened as she yanked the broom from my hand. "*Anak*, do you want to make us all poor?" she whispered. For years, I was convinced that sweeping after dark could somehow make all our money vanish.

At a young age, I learned about the power of *puwera usog*, a phrase used to ward off envy or a curse that might arise from excessive admiration. If a relative or friend exclaimed, 'Ay, you're so pretty!' they would usually follow it with, 'Puwera usog!'—an automatic incantation meant to protect against an accidental hex. When Carlota, the eldest Peñafiel daughter, had her first child, a family friend came to visit, gushing over his cuteness and showering Mama Doray with compliments about her adorable grandson. However, she didn't say the 'magic words.' About an hour later, the baby became fussy and began crying inconsolably. 'It's the usog,' Mama Doray declared knowingly, insisting that our visitor rub the baby's belly with a touch of her saliva and say puwera usog to 'reverse' the bad energy.

As I grew older and became more "sophisticated," I didn't cling to superstitions as much. Looking back now, I realize these beliefs did more than just make me cautious around the supernatural; they kept me connected to my culture and taught me to value family traditions. The myths and superstitions, passed down through generations, filled my childhood with humor and a sense of magic—something easily forgotten as adults in the modern world we live in. Though I may not believe in every superstition anymore, a part of me still whispers tabi po now and then, just in case.

6 Leaving Cebu

The Peñafiels were fairly well-known among the well-to-do and well-connected in Cebu, and Papa Emilio was the heart of the family's reputation. With his tailored suits, fedora, and polished shoes, he moved through the streets as if he owned every cobblestone beneath him—which, in a way, he did, at least those near his store. Papa Emilio and his partners, Señors Buada and Castro, ran a hardware store on Colon Street, a place always bustling with merchants and bargaining customers. Educated at the prestigious Ateneo de Manila, he spoke both Spanish and English fluently, though his true gift was his way with people. He had a natural charm, always knowing just the right thing to say to make others feel as if they were the most important person in the room. Whether mingling with the business elite or sharing a joke with street vendors, he fit in everywhere. For him, every social gathering was a stage, and Cebu's small but tightly knit society was his audience.

Papa's social skills were both a blessing and a curse. His ease in connecting with people from all walks of life undoubtedly contributed to the store's success, but they also played a role in his eventual downfall. His partners grew increasingly frustrated as they watched him prioritize mingling with vendors and customers over handling the daily demands of the business. They resented his tendency to offer generous discounts to boost his social standing—a habit that began to hurt the store's bottom line. Papa's charm, it turned out, sometimes came at a cost.

Buada and Castro spoke with Papa repeatedly, and each time he promised to improve. However, whatever efforts he made were ultimately token gestures, intended more to placate his partners than to address their concerns. Eventually, Buada and Castro had enough and decided to buy Papa Emilio out of his share of the business. Although Papa protested, their decision was final—it was, after all, for the good of the business.

Papa was devastated. The store had been more than just the family's sole source of income—it was a part of his identity, a symbol of his success, and a reflection of his place in the community. Facing his high-society friends after being forced out of the business he'd built from the ground up filled him with shame. Word traveled quickly in those circles, and Papa couldn't bear the thought of living in a city where he was no longer part of its elite.

I was about eight years old when I overheard him break the news to Mama Doray. They were in the living room, the door slightly ajar. I heard them speaking in English—the language they used when they didn't want me to understand. They thought I couldn't follow it, but I kept my comprehension a secret, finding an advantage in playing dumb.

"We have to move to Manila."

"What? Why?" she asked.

He explained the situation: Buada and Castro's frustration with his easy-going approach to business, and their decision to buy him out of his stake in the store. Mama Doray was furious.

She scolded him for being irresponsible, reminding him that she'd warned him that his showing off and arrogance would catch up to him one day—and now that day had arrived.

Papa Emilio remained silent. What could he say?

"So, what now?" she demanded.

Papa explained that he had some prospective opportunities in Luzon. Moving back to Manila would give him a fresh start and a chance to rebuild.

"What about Ging?" Mama Doray asked. "I suppose we could take her with us," she added, answering her own question.

When Mama Doray broke the news to me, she put a more positive spin on it. We had to move to Manila, she explained, because Papa Emilio had found another job. She added that Manila was a bigger city with more things to do and better opportunities for the whole family.

I didn't fully understand what she meant with all that, but the idea of moving to a new city sounded exciting. At the time, I didn't think about being separated from my biological family. Up until then, I had spent the majority of my life with the Peñafiels, so it only seemed natural that I would go with them if they moved—just as I had when we moved from Sikatuna to Logarta.

Mama Doray knew she would encounter resistance from Mama Caring, who had been reluctant even to let me move to Logarta. She certainly wouldn't agree to the Peñafiels taking me to Manila. So Mama Doray did something underhanded—she proposed the idea to my father's mother, Lola Julia.

Lola Julia was a remnant of the Spanish colonial era. Born in Comillas, Spain, she was betrothed to my grandfather Jose (my father's namesake), who worked for *La Tabacalera*, the first and oldest cigar factory in Asia. She met Jose for the first time when she arrived in Cebu to be married, and it was there they settled to raise a family.

She never learned to speak *Visayan*, the dialect of Cebu. Like many Spaniards of her time, she saw no need to learn Tagalog or regional dialects, as Spanish was the official language of the Philippines. Unless you were a missionary, there was little reason to learn the local languages.

As a product of her generation, Lola Julia carried an air of superiority, and Mama Caring always felt that this attitude created a rift between them. During our visits to Lola Julia's home on her birthday, she was never as warm or welcoming to us as she was to the families of her other children. Mama Caring also sensed that Lola

Julia didn't fully respect her—a lack of respect that was evident in how she interfered with the decision about my move to Manila.

Lola Julia knew the Peñafiels from when they lived on Sikatuna Street. Emilio was a well-respected business owner, known throughout the community. Doray often accompanied him to social events among Cebu's elite, and she was friends with Señora Teresa "Chichay" Escaño, heiress to the Escaño Shipping Lines fortune. And they spoke Spanish—an indicator of being "educated" Filipinos in Lola Julia's eyes.

When the Peñafiels told Lola Julia they were moving to Manila and wanted to take me with them, she thought it was a wonderful idea, believing it would be a great opportunity for young Ging. The Peñafiels were a cultured and respectable family; I would be in good hands.

With Lola Julia's blessing, they visited Mama Caring with their proposal. She wasn't happy about it and felt like she was being ambushed.

"Ging will be so far away. I barely get to see her enough as it is," Mama Caring protested.

"Caring, don't be so selfish," responded Lola Julia. "It will be good for the girl. Besides, you have six other children."

Mama Caring felt insulted.

"My children are not puppies to be given away. It doesn't matter how many I have."

Lola Julia looked over at my father.

"What do you think Jose? Wouldn't this move be a great opportunity for your daughter?"

My father, who had remained silent until that point, responded.

"Well, yes. Caring, this move to Manila would be good for Ging."

Mama Caring felt defeated. She was outnumbered, and no amount of protest would change their minds. Reluctantly, she allowed the Peñafiels to take me with them to Manila.

Mama Caring wanted to keep me close, but her timid nature was easily overshadowed by the assertive and unyielding forces of Mama

Doray and Lola Julia. Mama Doray saw herself as my primary caretaker, firmly believing that I would thrive under her guidance. This emotional tug-of-war weighed heavily on my heart, creating a struggle between the quiet yearning for my birth mother's embrace and the authoritative presence of my adoptive mother, a woman who had become an integral part of my life. Their competing influences wove a complex web of affection and conflict, one that shaped my identity in ways I was only beginning to understand.

7 Manila Bound

The weeks leading up to our departure were a blur, scarcely remembered in the haze of excitement and anxiety. Days blended together as the Peñafiels sorted through their household, packing everything for the move to Luzon. Before I knew it, departure day had arrived.

We arrived at the ferry terminal in the early morning. I felt a thrill at the thought of living in a new place and seeing Manila for the first time—it was an adventure. Yet beneath that excitement was a deep sadness, knowing I wouldn't see my family, especially my Mama Caring, as often as before.

Mama Caring and my sister Helen met us at the terminal to see us off. Mama handed me a small bag of candies for the long trip. I thanked her, though I couldn't quite look up; a quick glance told me she had tears welled up in her eyes.

A few steps behind, the Peñafiels approached. "It's time, Ging. We should start boarding," Mama Doray said gently, reaching out to touch Mama Caring's arm.

"We'll take good care of her, Caring—don't you worry," she reassured.

Mama Caring, struggling to keep a brave face, only managed a silent nod. Helen pulled me into a hug, pressing a soft kiss to my forehead. "Study hard in school, Ging," she whispered.

Then came the moment I'd been dreading: Mama Caring's turn to say goodbye. She knelt to face me, her gentle features heavy with sorrow. Her hands cupped my face, fingers brushing my cheeks, lingering—as if to memorize every detail. I felt tears on her fingertips, though she kept her expression as calm as she could.

"Promise me you'll be good, Ging," she said, her voice trembling. "And that you won't forget about us."

I nodded, unable to utter a word.

"You'll enjoy living in Manila," she said, her voice barely a whisper. "I'll come to visit you soon." But the look on her face told me that even she didn't know when "soon" would be. The future was uncertain, and I could see her heart already aching from the distance that would grow between us.

The final boarding call rang out. Mama Doray held out her hand, signaling for me to join her and Papa Emilio up the ramp. Mama Caring's tear-filled eyes stayed fixed on me, her brave smile beginning to falter. I took Mama Doray's hand and, together with Papa Emilio, moved toward the boat.

Once on board, I turned to look back one last time. Mama Caring stood on the dock, her small figure framed by the early morning light, her hand raised in a gentle wave. I pressed against the railing, trying to memorize her face: the warmth in her eyes, her comforting smile. Even from a distance, I could see the tears slipping down her cheeks, catching the sunlight.

As the ferry pulled away, I continued watching her until she was just a speck on the dock. And even as Cebu disappeared behind me, Mama Caring's image remained sharp in my mind, her promise that we would see each other soon echoing in my ears.

8 New Life In Manila

Upon our arrival in Manila, we temporarily lodged with relatives of Papa Emilio. The cramped quarters were a stark contrast to the spacious house we had left behind in Cebu. The tight living space was often overwhelming, and the lack of privacy served as a constant reminder of how much our lives had changed. Mama Doray frequently voiced her discomfort, her frustration palpable in the way she tidied endlessly or sighed after yet another crowded mealtime. Yet we endured it, reminding ourselves that this arrangement was only temporary—a stepping stone to a new chapter in our lives.

After a few weeks, Papa Emilio found a comfortable house to rent in the San Juan neighborhood. It was modest but welcoming, with enough space for our family to breathe again. That house would become our sanctuary for the next several years—a place where I would learn to navigate this new life, separated from Mama Caring and my siblings, but filled with hope for a promising future.

For Mama Doray, the house was a source of renewed energy. She was delighted to have her own space again and wasted no time transforming it into a proper home. Curtains were hung, furniture arranged, and the scent of her cooking soon filled the air. It didn't take long for her to make the house feel warm and familiar, as though we had always lived there. Her pride in our new home softened the edges of our transition, making it easier for us all to embrace this new start in Manila.

As we got settled in San Juan, I was anxious to explore our new surroundings. Mama Doray and Papa Emilio had told me so much about Manila from their years living here before moving to Cebu. Manila was known as the "Pearl of the Orient," and while Cebu had its charm, Manila in the late 1930s was a dazzling metropolis—vibrant, alive, and brimming with possibilities. I couldn't wait to experience it for myself.

Papa Emilio wasted no time introducing me to the wonders of his old haunts. On weekends, he would take me on long walks through downtown Manila. We often began at Plaza Goiti, a bustling square alive with activity and the melodic clang of bells from passing *tranvías*. I was mesmerized the first time I saw a tranvía. This electric tram system, one of the most advanced in Asia at the time, seemed like something out of a storybook. I'll never forget my first ride. Stepping onto the tranvía felt like boarding a magical carriage that whisked me through the vibrant heart of the city. The rattling of the tracks, the metallic chime of the conductor's bell, and the rush of wind through the open sides filled me with wonder. Clutching Papa Emilio's hand tightly, I watched the lively streets of downtown Manila unfurl before me, my eyes wide with excitement.

Rizal Avenue was another favorite. The avenue had an energy of its own, with people from all walks of life milling about. Men in *barongs* and suits strolled the sidewalks alongside women dressed in the latest fashions from Escolta's high-end boutiques. You could hear people speaking in Tagalog, Spanish, Chinese, English, and even German. It was here that I first realized how diverse Manila truly was. There were Chinese merchants, former Spanish colonialists, American businessmen, and Japanese artisans. I marveled at the languages I heard, the snippets of stories unfolding all around me.

Escolta Street was where Papa Emilio's connections seemed endless, introducing me to unforgettable people who left lasting impressions on my childhood. Among them was Ma Mon Luk, the genial owner of the famous Chinese restaurant. He greeted us with a warm smile whenever my father brought me along, and I always ran to him with a big hug, as if he were a favorite uncle. Mr. Ma would chuckle and ask, "What will it be today?" though he already knew my answer: his famous *siopao*!

The steamed pork buns were one of his specialties, alongside his renowned *mami* noodle soup. With a twinkle in his eye, he would take my hand and lead me to a tray of freshly steamed siopao, letting me choose one. I cherished that small act of kindness, and the first bite never failed to delight me. The bun's pillowy softness and savory filling felt like a little piece of heaven. Afterward, I always thanked him with another big hug, my heart as full as my belly.

Then there was Tom Pritchard, the charismatic owner of Tom's Dixie Grill. Tom was unlike anyone I had ever met—tall, with dark skin that seemed to glow under the restaurant's warm lights, and an exuberant laugh that could fill the entire room. He was the first Black American I had ever encountered, and he fascinated me. Papa Emilio told me that Tom had once been a US Army soldier, posted to the Philippines during the Spanish-American War. After his tour of duty, he chose to remain in the Philippines, marrying a Filipina and eventually opening his immensely popular restaurant.

Tom's Dixie Grill was more than just a dining establishment—it was a place of wonder for me, a portal to a world of flavors I had never known. On special occasions, Papa Emilio would take our family there, and it always felt like a celebration. The meals were unlike anything I had tasted before: plates of crispy fried chicken, buttery biscuits, and creamy mashed potatoes smothered in rich, savory gravy. Papa would explain that this was Southern American cuisine, and I savored every bite with wide-eyed delight.

Tom always made time to visit our table, greeting us with his booming voice and catching up with Papa Emilio like old friends. He would tease me about how much I loved his cooking, his broad smile making me feel instantly at ease. His kindness made me feel special, like we were more than just guests in his restaurant. In those moments, it felt as though we were part of a larger family, connected by laughter, good food, and stories shared over a table.

Those early days in Manila were some of the happiest of my life. It was a city of dreams, and for a little girl from Cebu, it was a world that promised endless adventures. Papa Emilio's hand was always warm and steady as we explored, his deep voice filling my ears with stories of the city's history and its bright future. The Pearl of the Orient glimmered all around me, and I was lucky enough to bask in its light.

9 Dinalupihan

Not long after we settled in Manila, Papa Emilio accepted a position managing the La Mitra rice plantation in Dinalupihan, a quiet municipality in the province of Bataan. It was far from the San Juan district of Manila where we took up residence after moving from Cebu. Papa's work at the plantation demanded his presence most of the time, so he did not live with us in San Juan. He spent most of the year in Dinalupihan, coming back to Manila only on weekends or during special occasions.

Papa didn't own the plantation, but many of the locals assumed he did. Papa Emilio was the manager, not the *haciendero*, but in those days, the line between ownership and management was blurred in the eyes of the workers. He carried himself with quiet authority and innate dignity, so people naturally afforded him the same respect and deference they would the landowner himself. It didn't matter to them that the real owner was an absentee landlord who lived in Manila, seldom visiting the estate. For all intents and purposes, Papa Emilio was the haciendero.

Papa lived in Dinalupihan for most of the year, overseeing the day-to-day operations of the plantation. His role as manager kept him busy from dawn until dusk, supervising the tenant farmers and ensuring the land was properly tended. Papa's position was precarious—caught between the absentee landowners above and the tenant farmers below, each with their own demands and expectations. He took pride in his work, but I could see the toll it took on him. The long hours and the responsibility of managing the plantation weighed on him, though he rarely spoke of it. When he came home to San Juan on the weekends, he always looked tired but greeted us with a smile, seemingly content to have a brief respite from the plantation.

Mama Doray and I only visited the plantation during the summer months. Those visits became the highlight of my childhood, as they were a time when we could all be together as a family in a place that seemed like a world away from Manila. We would make the long trip from the city in Papa's car, the roads becoming narrower and more uneven as we left behind Manila's clamor and ventured deeper into the heart of the province.

When we arrived at the plantation, the change in atmosphere was palpable. City sounds dissolved into the rustling of rice paddies and the distant cries of birds—a softer, slower rhythm that seemed to breathe differently. The plantation was immense, stretching as far as the eye could see, with emerald-green fields shimmering under the sun. I had never seen such wide-open spaces before; it felt as if the land itself was endless. The air in Dinalupihan was different from the city—cleaner, fresher, tinged with the scent of growing rice, sugarcane, corn, and the occasional hint of smoke from the workers' cooking fires.

When I first laid eyes on the plantation house in Dinalupihan, I was equally awestruck. It was nothing like our home in San Juan. The house was a grand, old structure with wide windows, high ceilings, and large wooden floors that creaked with every step. Majestic yet weathered, the house exuded a faded grandeur that whispered of its Spanish colonial past. Some of the locals referred to it as *Casa Grande*.

The summer visits to Dinalupihan felt like grand adventures. The wide-open spaces of the province were so inviting—far less confined than our neighborhood in San Juan. I was eager to explore this new environment. To keep me out of trouble, Papa enlisted a teenage boy named Mateo to be my companion and guardian. Mateo was a kind-hearted soul, always ready to indulge my whims, even when they bordered on mischief.

One of my favorite pastimes was climbing the enormous *narra* tree that stood proudly beside the plantation house. Its thick branches stretched out like welcoming arms, and I imagined it as my fortress in the sky, a secret realm where I ruled over the fields below. I would scramble up its rough bark, feeling the rush of exhilaration as I climbed to the top. From my perch high above, the world looked different—smaller and more magical. I would watch the workers moving through the fields, their figures small against the vibrant green backdrop, and I felt like a queen surveying my kingdom.

After descending from my lofty perch, I would race over to the mill, where huge piles of rice husks were stacked high, remnants of the day's work. The husks were coarse and rough against my skin, but I didn't care. I loved jumping around in the piles, diving into the heaps and sending clouds of dust swirling into the air. The itch from the husks was a small price to pay for the joy they brought—each dive a celebration of the carefree days of summer.

Yet the true highlight of my visits to Dinalupihan was always the *Flores de Mayo* Festival. Flores de Mayo is a month-long Catholic celebration held throughout the Philippines every May to honor the Virgin Mary. The pinnacle of the festival was the *Santacruzan*, the final procession at the end of the month. It was no ordinary parade, but a solemn pageant commemorating the discovery of the True Cross by Queen Helena, mother of Emperor Constantine.

For as long as I could remember, I had watched the Santacruzan from the sidelines, admiring the beauty and pageantry of it all. The procession always began at twilight, just as the day's heat softened into a balmy evening. The *Reynas*—each representing a different virtue or Marian title—marched through the streets in gowns that shimmered in the torchlight, accompanied by handsome escorts dressed in crisp barongs. They carried symbols of the Virgin Mary and the cross, while the rest of the town followed behind, singing hymns and lighting the way with candles.

The *Reyna Elena*, representing Queen Helena herself, was the centerpiece of the procession. She always wore the most elaborate gown, often in white or gold, her head crowned with a delicate tiara of pearls and flowers. Trailing behind her was a small boy dressed as Constantine, holding a cross aloft—symbolizing the triumph of Christianity.

During one of my visits to Dinalupihan, the festival organizers asked Papa Emilio if his beautiful mestiza daughter could participate in the celebration. Papa hesitated at first—his schedule was demanding—but seeing how much it meant to me, he relented.

I was ecstatic! Instead of watching from the sidelines, I would finally be part of the celebration. I had always imagined what it would be like to be one of the girls in the procession, to walk through the streets while everyone looked on with admiration. And now, here was my chance.

On the day of the Santacruzan, the whole town gathered in the plaza, buzzing with anticipation. The air was thick with the scent of incense and flowers, and the faint strains of church hymns floated through the streets. I stood at the front of the procession in a flowing white gown adorned with lace, my hair pinned up, and a tiara perched on my head. The gown's length made it difficult to walk, and the heat pressed down like a heavy blanket—but I didn't care. I felt like a princess.

The procession began at sunset, as the sky deepened into violet and the first stars blinked awake. We moved slowly through the streets, led by boys carrying tall torches, their flames flickering in the evening breeze. Behind me, the other Reynas followed, their gowns as elaborate as mine.

The crowd was enormous—men, women, and children from all over Dinalupihan and nearby towns had gathered. They lined the streets, holding candles and rosaries, their eyes fixed on us as we passed. The scent of freshly strung *sampaguita* garlands mingled with torch smoke, creating a heady mixture that hung in the air like a blessing.

I was almost mesmerized by the sights and sounds—so much so that I barely noticed the torchbearers drawing closer, their excitement making them careless. Papa, watching from the edge of the crowd, grew visibly uneasy as the flames danced dangerously near my gown. One of the boys stumbled, nearly brushing me with his torch. My heart began to race.

That's when Papa's voice rang out, sharp and clear. "Careful with those torches! Stay back!" His commanding voice left no room for argument.

Startled by his tone, the boys straightened up at once. Slightly embarrassed, they regained their composure and continued with the procession, but at a safer distance from me. Papa's scolding caused a brief stir—onlookers craned their necks, murmuring as they tried to make sense of the commotion. I was a little embarrassed for the boys and myself—this wasn't exactly the attention I was expecting. But very quickly the procession resumed without further incident.

And so I continued with the parade, feeling every bit like a princess as I walked with the other Reynas—it was like a dream come true. Every admiring glance, every whispered compliment felt like a tender embrace from the town itself. I basked in the attention, a little girl briefly transformed into a queen, swept into a tradition she had once only dreamed of.

The air buzzed with energy—a vibrant symphony of excited chatter, the rhythmic shuffle of a thousand feet, and the soaring hymns that seemed to lift us skyward. The sweet scent of freshly strung sampaguita garlands mingled with the earthy aroma of damp soil after a brief afternoon shower. From the food stalls lining the plaza came the savory aroma of grilled meats and the rich sweetness of sticky rice cakes. It was a feast for the senses—a living tapestry of torchlight, song, and flavor.

After the procession ended, Papa and I made our way to the food stalls, still in my gown, cheeks flushed from elation. In all the excitement, I hadn't realized that I had barely eaten all day and was now quite hungry. I devoured a stick of *inihaw na baboy*, the tender pork slightly charred and brushed with a sweet, garlicky glaze. Then came a serving of *puto* and *kutsinta*, the soft and sticky rice cakes, served warm on banana leaves. The flavors seemed richer that night, perhaps because everything—every bite, every breath—was colored by the glow of celebration. I drank a cold bottle of Coca-Cola, its fizz tickling my tongue, while firecrackers popped in the distance and a small band played upbeat folk music near the church steps.

Everywhere I looked, the townspeople were gathered—old and young, rich and poor, locals and visiting relatives. The whole town had come alive, as if each person had been awakened from a long slumber and invited to dance in the open air. Elderly women in *baro't saya*, a traditional Filipino dress ensemble, handed out sweets to children; teenagers laughed as they took turns on the makeshift ferris wheel beside the plaza. Even the local vendors had paused their bargaining to watch the festivities, clapping and singing along with the music. There was no division here—only one people, united in faith, joy, and pride. It was as though the heart of the town beat in unison, and for one perfect night, we all belonged to something larger than ourselves.

When the evening finally wound down, I could barely keep my eyes open. My feet ached from walking and standing, and my gown felt heavier now, weighed down by perspiration and dust. Papa hailed a *kalesa*, which took us back to the plantation house. During the ride, I drifted off from exhaustion, the chirping of crickets and the waning sounds of the fiesta wrapping around me like a lullaby.

Back home, Papa helped me get ready for much needed nighttime slumber. He tucked the blanket around me, and kissed my forehead gently.

"Good job, *mija*. You were the prettiest one out there," he whispered, smoothing a curl from my cheek.

I smiled sleepily, too tired to reply. Outside, the last echoes of the festival faded into the quiet hum of the countryside. Inside, I lay cocooned in warmth and pride, knowing that for one enchanted evening, I had not only walked in a procession—I had walked in a dream.

Looking back on the summers in Dinalupihan, I remember them as the happiest days in my childhood. Climbing the narra tree, playing in the rice husks, participating in the Flores de Mayo Festival—the memories remain vivid even with the passage of time. It was a time of joy and innocence, unaware of the shadows gathering in the distance. My world was still radiant and whole—a realm of celebration and light, untouched by the storm that would one day darken its horizon.

10 Mama Doray's Vices

There comes a time in every child's life when they realize their parents are less than perfect—that they're human, even flawed. I was about nine when I reached that realization with Mama Doray, and I began to see she was a study in contradictions.

Mama Doray was uncompromising in her Catholic devotion. She prayed the Rosary daily and attended Mass even when it wasn't Sunday. In our neighborhood, she was known as a woman of unwavering faith, her reputation beyond reproach.

With the others away at work, most days it was just the two of us at home. And in all that time together, I began to notice that Mama Doray had her little secrets.

In addition to her faith, she was also famous for her chorizo. Made from a closely guarded recipe, it was better than any sausage sold in the local markets. Neighbors, friends, relatives—even distant acquaintances—sought out her prized chorizo. Though she never shared the recipe, I knew it by heart. But I was sworn to secrecy.

One afternoon, while she was preparing a batch in the kitchen, I peeked around the doorway just in time to see her retrieve a bottle of clear liquid from the cupboard. She poured a measured amount into a small glass, inspected it carefully, then tipped it into the mixing bowl with the other ingredients. Afterward, she refilled the glass—but this time, she raised it to her lips and drank it in one swift swallow.

As she set the glass down, she caught sight of me in the doorway. A mischievous twinkle lit her eye.

"Ay, anak," she said, smiling. "The gin is my secret ingredient!"

I was old enough to know what alcohol was. Papa Emilio enjoyed a whiskey after dinner, and he made no attempt to hide it. But I wondered if he knew about Mama Doray's secret. She didn't drink otherwise—not with company, at least. She only drank with her chorizo. And she always insisted it was "for flavor."

Another time, I caught sight of Mama Doray performing what I later realized was a regular ritual.

I was outside playing when I noticed her in the bathroom, the window cracked open. Hidden behind a tree, I had a clear view—but she had no idea I was watching.

She stood in front of the mirror, wrapping a bandana tightly around her hair, glancing over her shoulder as if to make sure no one was watching. Then, she took a handful of cotton balls and began stuffing them into her mouth. I wondered—did she have a toothache?

What happened next shocked me.

She opened a pack of cigarettes, removed one, and placed it between her lips. With practiced ease, she struck a match and brought the flame to the tip of the cigarette. She inhaled deeply, then exhaled slowly, the smoke drifting away on the gentle afternoon breeze. Her expression softened into something like quiet satisfaction.

I was absolutely stunned—Mama Doray was smoking!

Papa Emilio smoked a pipe, and that always seemed perfectly normal to me. It was an ordinary habit for a man. But a woman smoking? That felt different. In my young mind, it was something only women who went to nightclubs did—the kind of women Mama Doray said needed more religion in their lives.

If the ladies from church had seen her, I was sure they would have clutched their rosaries in horror.

But there was something in her expression as she smoked—a quiet contentment, a momentary escape from the endless rhythm of housework and motherhood. It felt like a small rebellion, a guilty pleasure she allowed herself. Wasn't she entitled to that?

Just like her occasional sips of gin, I never told anyone. I became the silent guardian of her secret, sensing that some things were better kept between us.

Mama Doray's third vice was gambling—specifically *jueteng* (pronounced WHET-TENG), a local numbers game, something like an informal lottery. Though illegal, jueteng was—and still is—popular in the Philippines, especially among the poor and middle class. The buy-in was modest, but the promise of a big payout kept people playing, even if the odds weren't in their favor.

Of all her vices, jueteng was the one Mama Doray didn't bother to hide—at least not from me. In fact, it was something I got to participate in, in my own small way.

In jueteng, superstition often guided the choice of numbers. A chance encounter with a person or animal, a strange coincidence, even a mundane event—any of these could be interpreted as signs. Dreams, especially, were considered fertile ground for lucky numbers. That's where I came in.

Before the *kubrador*—the bet collector—made his rounds through the neighborhood, I'd tell Mama Doray about a dream I'd had the night before.

"Mama, last night I dreamt I had two goats. I sold them at the market and made a nice profit."

"Oh, anak! What color were the goats?"

"One white, one black."

"That is surely a sign of luck!"

She would then divine a number combination from the symbols in my dream. I never understood the logic behind her method, but she always seemed confident in her choices.

Most of my dreams were made up—crafted for her benefit—but they seemed to help. And more than anything, jueteng became something we shared. A small ritual. A quiet bond.

These small, daily vices were only fragments of her—flaws,

perhaps, but also clues to her true nature. In watching Mama Doray, vices and all, I began to understand that a person's public and private selves could diverge, sometimes sharply. Even mothers, I learned, are complicated—wrapped in quiet mysteries they guard like treasures.

Each time I caught her indulging in one of her secrets, it felt like I was unwrapping a gift meant only for me. A glimpse into the hidden folds of her life. And with every glimpse, I understood her in a way no one else ever would.

11 Sunday Mornings In Old Manila

In the Peñafiel household, Sunday was the Lord's day, and attending Mass was non-negotiable. Mama preferred the early service, when it was practically still dark outside. "Why do we have to go to church so early, Mama?" I'd ask, rubbing the sleep from my eyes.

"Because it gets so hot and crowded later," she'd say, her voice firm but patient. Then she'd add, "Our Savior Jesus Christ died for our sins, anak. Surely we can give up a little sleep to show our thanks."

I knew there was no point in protesting further; missing church was out of the question, and there was no chance she'd go to a later Mass.

Papa Emilio, however, didn't go with us. He preferred attending Mass at a different church, later in the morning. That was his choice, and Mama Doray never questioned it.

I was curious about this church Papa attended and even more curious why Mama didn't insist that he join us. One day, I finally asked him about it.

"Papa, which church do you go to on Sundays?"

"I attend Mass at San Agustin in *Intramuros*. It's a grand old church I used to attend as a boy."

I came up with an idea. Mama wouldn't let me skip church but maybe she would let me go with Papa.

"It sounds beautiful! Do you think I could go with you to San Agustin sometime?"

He smiled. "Why of course! I would love to show you the church and take you around Intramuros. It's full of history and there is so much to see."

I was sure Mama saw through my plan, but she agreed to let me go with him. As long as I was going to Mass, that's all that mattered to her.

The following Sunday, we took a taxi into the heart of old Manila for my first visit to Intramuros and San Agustin Church. At Papa Emilio's request, the taxi driver dropped us off a short distance from the church so we could take in the sights on foot.

Intramuros felt like a world apart—a walled city preserving Manila's oldest memories within its formidable fortifications. Spanish colonial architecture lined the cobblestone streets, where sturdy adobe houses with capiz shell windows glimmered in the daylight. Horse-drawn kalesas clattered along the lanes, ferrying visitors and locals through shaded, narrow streets. It was a city within a city, steeped in history, with every street corner whispering stories of a bygone era.

The surrounding walls, built from coral and adobe, stood tall and resolute, as if protecting the city's long-forgotten secrets. The gates, wide and imposing, marked the threshold between the past and present. Outside, modern Manila pulsed with relentless energy, but within Intramuros, time seemed suspended, cradled by the dignified quiet of weathered stones and secluded courtyards.

As we neared San Agustin Church, its imposing presence commanded my attention. It stood like a sentinel in the heart of Intramuros, its weathered, Baroque-style façade a testament to centuries of endurance. From intricately carved stonework to towering bell towers, every detail exuded resilience and grace. Papa Emilio remarked that San Agustin, having withstood earthquakes, war, and fires, embodied the strength and spirit of the Filipino people.

Inside, the church was as breathtaking as it was solemn. High, vaulted ceilings stretched toward the heavens, adorned with paintings of saints and angels gazing serenely down on the faithful. Morning sunlight streamed through stained glass windows, scattering vibrant colors across the cool stone floors. Marble statues stood in prayerful silence along the walls, while rows of heavy wooden pews faced the grand altar, adorned with gilded relics and sacred images.

When the organ played, its resonant notes filled the sanctuary, reverberating against the stone walls and stirring every heart. The music carried an almost otherworldly power, lifting spirits and immersing us in the profound beauty of the moment.

After Mass, Papa Emilio and I strolled through the cobblestone streets of Intramuros to a small neighborhood where the houses stood with heavy wooden doors, their dark wood gleaming with the polish of time. We arrived at a grand old house adorned with intricately carved shutters and a sweeping balcony—a relic of colonial splendor. This was the home of Doña Amparo, the woman who had raised Papa Emilio after he was orphaned.

Papa Emilio's mother had been a maid in Doña Amparo's household, but she tragically died giving birth to him. The wealthy Spanish lady, moved by compassion and seeing promise in the infant, took him in, sparing him from what could have been a life of neglect. A close friend of his mother, another Filipina maid named Maria, had recently given birth herself. With a nurturing heart, Maria became a second mother to Papa Emilio, nursing and caring for him during his tender early years.

As he grew, Doña Amparo—whom Papa affectionately called Madrina (Spanish for godmother)—ensured he was given every opportunity to thrive. She paid for his education and insisted he attend Ateneo de Manila, a prestigious Jesuit university. In her household, he learned to read, write, and speak both Spanish and English, becoming fluent in each—a living testament to the love and ambition of the woman who had chosen to elevate him from his humble beginnings.

Out of respect and gratitude, Papa Emilio visited Madrina Amparo every Sunday after Mass. On this first visit to Intramuros, I was to join him in honoring his godmother, continuing a cherished tradition.

When Papa introduced me, I greeted her in Spanish: "Doña Amparo, *encantada de conocerle*."

She was an older woman, her silver hair and lined face marked by the passage of time. Yet, despite her age, she retained a commanding grace and elegance that spoke of her once youthful beauty. She smiled warmly, her eyes glimmering with wisdom, and gently patted my head in acknowledgment.

As was his custom, Papa informed me he had bookkeeping tasks to assist Madrina Amparo with and instructed me to wait in the parlor. He reminded me to be on my best behavior and not to touch anything. "If you're good," he added with a knowing smile, "I'll take you for ice cream afterward." I nodded solemnly, determined to earn my treat.

The parlor felt like a portal to another era. Though instructed to remain quietly seated, curiosity got the better of me. The room was a treasure trove, almost like a small museum—paintings, sepia-toned photographs, and various curios filled the space, each a piece of her storied past. I wandered carefully, marveling at the artifacts that seemed to whisper stories of her life in Spain and her years in the Philippines.

When Papa returned, we bid our goodbyes to Doña Amparo, with a promise to visit again the following Sunday.

As promised, Papa treated me to a nearby café, a warm, inviting establishment filled with the rich aroma of freshly brewed espresso and sweet pastries. While he sipped a cold beer and read the newspaper, I savored a scoop of ice cream—a refreshing escape from the afternoon heat. This became our Sunday ritual: attending Mass at San Agustin, visiting Madrina Amparo, and a frozen treat at the café. Though simple, it felt grand to me—a perfect way to spend time with Papa Emilio.

But then, almost suddenly, our visits to Doña Amparo stopped. One Sunday, instead of heading to her house as we always had, we went straight to the café. Curious, I turned to Papa Emilio and asked why we weren't visiting Madrina Amparo. He looked at me with a mixture of sadness and resolve before explaining that she had moved back to Spain. He offered no further details, and I didn't press him. At that age, I was content enough to focus on the ice cream and the familiar comfort of our café visits.

Not long after, I overheard a hushed conversation between Mama Doray and Papa Emilio. Their voices carried a weight that I couldn't quite comprehend. Papa mentioned Doña Amparo's longtime driver, a Japanese man, and how he had advised her to return to Spain, with no further explanation. Mama's voice quivered as she asked, "Should we leave too?"

Papa Emilio's tone was calm, though tinged with uncertainty. "Everything will probably be fine," he reassured her. "And even if we had to—with all of us, where would we go?"

I didn't fully grasp what they were discussing, but the tremor in Mama's voice told me it was something significant. In the weeks that followed, an invisible tension settled over our household, an undercurrent of unease I couldn't ignore. Though no one spoke openly about it, even as a child, I could sense that something was wrong. That feeling of uncertainty lingered, like a dark cloud hanging over our lives.

Those Sundays with Papa Emilio—attending Mass at San Agustin, strolling through Intramuros, and enjoying ice cream at the café—had once been the highlight of my week. But after Doña Amparo's departure, passing her now-empty home cast a shadow over those outings. The sight of her abandoned house became a stark reminder of the unease that seemed to envelop our lives.

12 First Communion

The morning sun poured its golden rays through the sheer curtains of the living room window, casting a warm glow on the small altar that Mama Doray kept as a permanent fixture in our home. A statue of the Virgin Mary stood at its center, surrounded by smaller statues of saints, their painted faces gazing serenely upon us. Fresh flowers adorned the altar, their fragrance mingling with the day's sense of reverence. Today was a day of celebration—the Feast of the Immaculate Conception—one of the most significant days of the year for Catholics in the Philippines. Yet the excitement I felt had less to do with the Holy Day or the festive procession that would soon make its way through the streets. It was December 8, 1941, and I was finally to receive my First Holy Communion.

That morning, Mama Doray brushed my hair and dressed me in my best white dress, one she had made just for this special occasion. She stepped back, her eyes glistening with pride as she took in the sight of me. Hand in hand, we walked outside to the waiting taxi that would take us to the church, Our Lady of Loretto.

As the taxi rumbled through the streets, my emotions swirled—a blend of anticipation and a flicker of anxiety. This was my second attempt to receive First Communion. The previous year, I had failed to memorize The Ten Commandments and could not participate in the ceremony. I had carried the weight of Mama Doray's disappointment for months. The nuns at school had been kind, reassuring me that I could try again, but their words came with a clear message: I would have to wait. This year, however, was different. I had studied diligently, reciting the commandments until they felt as familiar as my own name. Today, I was ready.

When we arrived at Our Lady of Loretto, the world seemed to shine brighter. The other girls receiving the Sacrament, dressed in similar white dresses and veils, twirled around in delight, their laughter filling the air. The boys, sharp in their crisp white barongs and black trousers, greeted us with shy smiles. It was a gathering of innocence and beauty, a shared moment of faith and anticipation. All the parents, gathered outside the church, beamed with pride, their faces glowing like the morning sun, capturing the spirit of the day in their loving glances.

Inside the church, the atmosphere was grand, filled with the soft glow of candles and the melodious hum of the choir. As I knelt at the altar, my heart thumped wildly in my chest. When the moment came, I accepted the Holy Communion, the wafer resting lightly on my tongue, a sacred moment that bound me to my faith and to my family.

As the Mass drew to a close, a ripple of whispers moved through the congregation. At first, it was only a murmur—a few heads turned, then a few more, spreading like ink on water. People were leaning in close to one another, their voices hushed but urgent. I didn't understand what was happening but the tone and atmosphere among the adults told me something was terribly wrong.

"What's happening, Mama?" I asked, clutching her hand.

"Wait a moment, anak," she replied, her brow furrowed as she strained to catch the fragments of conversation around us.

Then the news broke, shattering the festive mood: Japanese forces had bombed Pearl Harbor. The announcement swept through the congregation like a cold wind, leaving shock and fear in its wake. Parents clung tightly to their children, their faces etched with worry. Some of the adults were crying—something I had rarely witnessed outside of funerals. The sight unnerved me.

I looked up at Mama Doray. Her usual calm seemed to waver, her eyes clouded with dread. In that instant, she no longer seemed like the strong protector I had always seen her as. Instead, she was a woman facing the stark uncertainty of a world suddenly thrown into chaos.

The warmth of the day dissipated, replaced by an eerie chill that settled over us all. The celebration of my First Holy Communion, a milestone I had anticipated for so long, now felt distant—overshadowed by the grim reality of war. The echoes of laughter faded, and all I could hear was the pounding of my heart, reminding me that while I had taken a step forward in faith, the world was poised to take us all down a path we could never have anticipated.

13 Meaning Of War

War. I knew the word, but it felt distant, like something abstract—unreal and far removed from my life. In school, we had read about wars—battles fought and ended long ago. I had heard stories of suffering, of people forced to hide or fight, but they felt like tales from old books or fragments captured in faded photographs.

My only tangible connection to war was through Mama Doray's mother, Lola Sima.

Lola Sima had lived through two wars: the Philippine Revolution against Spanish colonists and the Philippine-American War. She rarely spoke about those times, but from Mama Doray, I learned she had lost her husband, a brother, and a son to the conflicts. Yet, even with this family history, war felt like a relic of the past, something that could never touch my present.

But now, the word carried a new, ominous weight. It was on the lips of every adult, laden with suffocating fear and unspoken anxieties. Conversations that once revolved around the weather, daily routines, or neighborhood gossip had vanished. Instead, the air was thick with worry—an all-consuming preoccupation with war and what it might mean for our safety and survival.

As I struggled to understand the meaning of war, I recalled a movie Mama Doray had taken me to see a few months earlier: *The*

Littlest Rebel, starring my favorite actress, Shirley Temple. In the film, Shirley plays a little girl caught in the turmoil of the American Civil War. While her father is away fighting the Union Army, their family home is overrun by the enemy, forcing her, her mother, and one of their slaves to flee into the woods during a rainstorm. Her mother falls ill and dies, and although she is briefly reunited with her father, he is soon captured and taken away.

I remembered crying in my seat, clutching Mama's hand as Shirley's face crumpled with sorrow on the screen. It was heartbreaking, and even though I knew it was only a movie, it had stayed with me.

But by the end of the film, Shirley had danced her way back into her father's arms, and the screen lit up with joy and song. The pain and loss melted away like a bad dream, replaced by laughter and dancing. Everything had turned out okay.

Now, surrounded by fear and uncertainty, I clung to a fragile, desperate hope: maybe this war, too, would play out like the movie. Just like Shirley's character, we would have to be brave. Sure, we'd have to endure sadness and hardship for a time, but in the end, we'd find our way back to joy. After all, I thought, didn't stories always end well if you kept believing? For now, that was the hope I held onto, clutching it close like the promise of a brighter day.

14 Arrival

The days immediately following the bombing of Pearl Harbor were surreal. Markets, usually bustling and noisy, were even more so now, with a different sense of urgency in the air. Families like ours rushed to stockpile food and supplies, quickly emptying store shelves. People hurried in the streets, clutching baskets filled with rice, dried fish, canned goods—whatever they could find. They bought as much as they could afford, then scrambled to trade with neighbors for more. It was a peculiar sight; like the preparations for a grand party but without any of the usual merriment.

Everyone was saying the war wouldn't last long. "A few months," they predicted, maybe a year. Some speculated it would end before the next monsoon season. But that did nothing to ease the fear. Manila, once vibrant and full of life, began to change. Shops closed early, with some never reopening. Soldiers, a familiar sight even before the war, now patrolled the streets armed with rifles. Where they once wore smiles, anticipating lively nights out on the town, their faces had turned grim, braced for the looming conflict.

Updates on the war began to trickle in. We learned that just hours after their attack on Pearl Harbor, the Japanese launched an assault on the Philippines. The initial aerial bombardment of key military targets was followed days later by landings of ground troops to the north and south of Manila.

Filipinos held on to the hope that our military, fighting alongside the US Army, led by General Douglas MacArthur, would protect our islands and repel the Japanese invaders. But that hope quickly dimmed.

Significantly outnumbered, US and Filipino troops withdrew to the Bataan Peninsula and to the island of Corregidor, situated at the entrance to Manila Bay. To spare Manila from destruction, it was declared an "Open City." Unfortunately, this did little to keep the Japanese from bombing the city in advance of their arrival. In addition to striking military targets, Japanese bombers hit civilian structures, including the Church of Santo Domingo within the walls of Intramuros. This historical landmark, founded by the Dominicans in 1587, was almost entirely destroyed. Priceless relics and church documents perished in the ensuing fires. Ironically, the Japanese failed to hit any of the ships in the nearby Pasig River, their intended targets. On January 2, 1942, the Japanese Army entered Manila, parts of the city still smoldering from the bombings. It was the beginning of the occupation.

The arrival of the Japanese army in Manila was almost anti-climactic. Neighborhood leaders aligned with the interim provisional government encouraged residents to welcome our new "visitors," even handing out small Japanese flags. Out of curiosity, I wanted to watch the procession, but Mama Doray forbade it. Later, some neighborhood kids who attended told me what they had seen.

The soldiers marched through the streets with an air of forced civility. They were neatly dressed in their uniforms and clean-shaven. Although the soldiers carried weapons, they seemed almost non-threatening. Some of them even waved and passed out candy to children lining the streets. It sounded more like a performance than a conquest. Hearing these accounts, I began to wonder if these invaders might not be as bad as everyone feared. That impression, however, didn't last long.

15 Illusion Of Normalcy

The first couple of months after the Japanese arrived seemed, on the surface, almost normal. Fear lingered like a shadow in the background, but life still felt strangely bearable. The soldiers patrolled the streets, mostly keeping to themselves in those early weeks, as if they too were adjusting to the new rhythm. Mama Doray insisted we act as though nothing had changed. I still accompanied her to the market, though prices had begun to climb and certain goods had quietly vanished from the stalls.

Nena and Tito tried to hold on to their routines. At first, they dressed each morning in their usual office attire and reported to their workplaces, but the American companies that employed them had shuttered almost overnight. The Japanese military wasted no time seizing the assets of Western and Filipino businesses, including land and buildings. Familiar English signs disappeared, replaced with foreign, unreadable *kanji*.

Their American bosses and co-workers—some of whom I remembered from office picnics I'd attended with Nena and Tito—were suddenly gone. Rumors spread that they'd been taken to Santo Tomas, a university turned into an internment camp. At the time, we knew little about what went on inside, only that its "residents" could not leave and were guarded by Japanese soldiers.

At night, Papa Emilio still played solitaire, but now it seemed he was only moving cards, not truly playing the game. Mama Doray busied herself with cooking and mending, her hands moving more from habit than from purpose. I swept the floor twice a day, even when it didn't need it—just to stay occupied. It felt as if we were all pretending. Pretending that if we clung to our habits tightly enough, the world wouldn't come apart.

In those early days of the occupation, I found a small silver lining in the looming dark cloud. The Catholic school I attended, Our Lady of Loreto, had closed its doors. Though the Japanese allowed some public schools to remain open, Mama Doray decided it was best for me to stay home. I didn't mind in the least. I had never been what you would call a model student, nor had I much interest in academic pursuits. To me, the closure felt less like a loss and more like an unexpected holiday.

Still, staying home meant missing the camaraderie of my classmates. Some of the neighborhood kids had started attending reopened public schools, and I was curious. I asked them what it was like under the Japanese.

The biggest difference, they said, was that anything related to America was strictly forbidden. Some of the old textbooks were still in use, but pages with pictures or references to America had been torn out or pasted together. To eliminate what they considered the corrupting influence of Western culture, the Japanese removed subjects such as history and literature. In their place, the new curriculum emphasized mathematics, science, the Japanese language, and cultural indoctrination.

To fill the gap left by the banned subjects, students were taught handicrafts like watercolor painting and *mizuhiki* knot tying, along with practical skills such as gardening. Some of the neighbor kids proudly showed me their notebooks filled with Japanese characters and the ornate knots they'd learned to tie. I was genuinely intrigued—and a little envious.

This wasn't at all like the school I was used to. No dull history lessons filled with names, dates, and places I struggled to remember.

Sure, there was still math—another least favorite—but there were hands-on activities that sounded fun. I even heard that on some days, their teachers, most of whom were Japanese, led them outside for group calisthenics. Imagine that: fresh air and movement instead of sitting in a stuffy classroom. Maybe Mama Doray would let me go.

"Mama, I heard some of the public schools are open and the neighbor kids are attending. Maybe I should go too so I don't fall behind."

"Absolutely not!" she responded, her voice sharp with conviction. She crossed her arms, as if to shield me from the very idea. "I don't care what the neighborhood kids are doing—you will not be attending a school taught by the Japanese!"

"But Mama, they're teaching math, science, and practical subjects like gardening and crafts."

"The answer is still no, and I don't want to hear another word of it!"

I was disappointed. I thought for sure she'd prefer I be in school rather than stuck at home doing busy-work chores. And I didn't want to fall behind. But Mama Doray was resolute. Her word was final.

Not long after, something happened that made me think perhaps she was right.

Mama and I were returning home from church when we saw a commotion in front of the school. One of the boys from our neighborhood—Francisco, though we all called him Cisco—was being berated by a Japanese soldier. Cisco stood frozen, his face pale, trying to explain himself in a flurry of apologies. But the soldier's expression was hard and unmoved.

Without warning, the soldier pulled out a bamboo switch and barked an order. Cisco turned around slowly, trembling. Then came the first strike. The switch sliced through the air with a whistle and landed with a sharp crack. Cisco cried out. Another strike. Then another. Each blow seemed louder than the last, echoing off the school walls.

I wanted to look away, but couldn't. My feet felt cemented to the ground, frozen in shock and fear, my eyes locked on the cruel scene unfolding before me.

After five strikes, the soldier finally stopped. Still yelling, the fury in his voice unmistakable, he motioned for Cisco to leave. Cisco turned, tears streaming down his face, and ran down the street, his sobs fading into the distance.

Mama gripped my hand tightly. I could feel her trembling.

She quickly pulled me by my arm, snapping me out of my trance, as we hurried back home.

Later, I learned what Cisco's "egregious" offense had been: he hadn't bowed low enough when passing the soldier.

I was shaken. Even the nuns, strict as they were, had never been so cruel. In that moment, everything changed. Any lingering hope that the Japanese had come in peace vanished, replaced by a stark reality. I was beginning to understand what it truly meant to live under occupation.

16 Losses Of War

By the fall of 1942, like many Filipino families, we began to feel the tightening grip of occupation. The Japanese forces, now more assertive, turned their attention to controlling the food supply. Checkpoints appeared along the main roads, manned by grim-faced soldiers whose eyes scanned every cart and truck. Vehicles from the provinces—once brimming with vegetables, fish, and sacks of rice—were halted, searched, and stripped of goods. Soldiers seized whatever they deemed necessary, leaving little for the markets of Manila. The crackdown fractured the supply chain, and the foods we once took for granted slowly vanished from our tables.

In response to the growing scarcity, the Japanese authorities introduced a rationing system to regulate access to staple goods. Each household received a ration card, its allotment determined by the number of family members. These cards dictated how much food or fuel a family could purchase within a given period. Civilians were required to carry their cards at all times and present them upon request. Local distribution centers were set up, often in schoolyards or public squares, where long lines formed as people waited to claim their share.

These long lines soon became a source of frustration and a growing sense of futility. At first, I accompanied Tito to the distribution center, ready to help carry our rations. We knew the crowds would be thick, so we woke before dawn, hoping to get ahead. The early morning cool was a small mercy. But when we arrived, the line already stretched for blocks—agitated men and women hoping to secure much needed food for their families. This routine became a ritual of disappointment. No matter how early we got up, we could never beat the swelling crowds. Eventually, demand outpaced supply, and the allotted goods began to dwindle. Soon, a single person could carry our meager rations with one arm, and it no longer made sense for both of us to go.

During the occupation, many families, including ours, faced the harsh reality of reduced—or nonexistent—income. Several months into the war, no one in the Peñafiel household held a job. We survived on the pooled life savings of the adult family members, watching its value diminish with each passing week. The Japanese military had banned US currency; possession of it could lead to severe punishment. In its place, they issued paper notes that became the legal tender throughout the Philippines. The conversion rates were dismal, but to buy anything—including rationed goods—we had no choice but to exchange our pre-war currency for occupation scrip.

Rationed items, when available, were priced in the Japanese-issued bills. The occupation government published official prices for essentials—rice, salt, kerosene—in the newspapers. But these prices were rarely honored. Costs soared, and families had to accept the stark truth of paying more for less. As the war dragged on, the Japanese currency came to be known as "Mickey Mouse Money"—a bitter nickname that captured its rapid descent into worthlessness. By 1943, inflation was so severe that items costing a bag of bills one week might cost double or triple the next. We learned to count value not in bills, but in bowls of rice.

The Japanese stranglehold on the supply chain affected more than just food—it also cut off access to medicines and medical care. With many doctors, nurses, and hospitals commandeered by the Japanese military, Filipino civilians were left to fend for themselves, often relying on ineffective herbal or traditional remedies.

This couldn't have come at a worse time for the Peñafiel family. Nena had always been prone to illness, especially respiratory troubles. Mama Doray used to say she was delicate, and the creeping malnutrition from our limited diet only made things worse.

It began with fatigue and shortness of breath. Nena, always helpful around the house, could barely sweep a few feet without needing to rest. She brushed it off at first. "Maybe there's something going around." Within days, her cough worsened—phlegmy, mucus-filled, relentless. Soon she couldn't get out of bed. Her fever burned like the midday sun, and she shivered through bouts of sweating and chills. Mama Doray stayed by her side, placing damp towels on her forehead. Tito and I took turns fanning her with an *abaniko* (woven palm hand fan). Without medicine, all we could do was pray.

I overheard Mama Doray speaking with our neighbor, Aling Rosa, about Nena's condition.

"She might have *pulmonya*," Rosa said quietly. She had lost a son to it the year before.

"Once the lungs fill with water…" Her voice trailed off.

Her eyes filled with tears as she clutched Mama Doray's hand. She didn't need to finish her sentence.

Nena's condition quickly deteriorated. Mama Doray called for the local priest to administer last rites. We gathered around Nena's bed and prayed the Rosary. Her eyes stayed open most of the time, her gaze glassy and far away.

Nena died just before dawn. It was summer, and the monsoon winds howled outside—but not loud enough to drown out Mama Doray's anguished sobbing.

I helped Mama prepare and dress Nena for burial. At that point in the war, the cemeteries had not yet been overwhelmed. We held a simple ceremony and returned home in silence.

Nena was our first casualty of the war.

17 Zonas

Our small neighborhood in San Juan, once a quiet enclave of modest homes, had turned into a place of guarded whispers and watchful eyes. Under Japanese occupation, the air itself felt heavy—suffocating—as if the joy from our lives before the war was being slowly drained, one breath at a time. Though the battlefields lay far from us, the war pressed in from all sides, its weight growing more unbearable by the day. Our homes, once sanctuaries of peace and security, now felt exposed, overrun. Nothing punctuated this transformation more than the *zonas*.

Zonas were a tactic employed by the *Kempeitai*—the feared secret police of the Imperial Japanese Army—designed to sever the lifeline between guerrilla fighters and members of the local populace who provided food, supplies, and shelter. Entire neighborhoods were cordoned off, transformed into tightly controlled search "zones."

The Japanese didn't always use zonas as a tactic to gain compliance of the Filipino people. At first, they relied on propaganda—an attempt to "win hearts and minds" and portray their invasion as a liberation from Western imperialism. It was part of their sweeping vision for the "Greater East Asia Co-Prosperity Sphere," a supposed union of Asian nations built on the promise of shared destiny and independence. But beneath the slogans lay a stark reality: the Philippines, long shaped by American influence, was not easily swayed. English was spoken in schools, Hollywood films played in theaters, and many Filipinos—while critical of colonial rule—recognized the Co-Prosperity Sphere for what it was: a thinly veiled power grab that served Japan far more than its so-called partners.

By late 1942, as the Filipino guerrilla resistance grew bolder and more organized, the Kempeitai began to shift tactics. Propaganda alone could no longer pacify the population. The Japanese had underestimated the resolve of these fighters. They began to realize that this ill-equipped, ragtag group had become something far more dangerous than a nuisance. They were now a direct threat to the occupation itself.

The zonas were sudden and unrelenting. Entire blocks would be cordoned off by Japanese soldiers, their harsh voices slicing through the morning air as they herded everyone—men, women, children, even the elderly—into the town plaza or a wide street. They claimed these raids were for our safety, a way to root out criminal elements threatening law and order. But we knew better.

Because zonas required significant manpower, they were anything but discreet. We often sensed when one was coming, though not always which neighborhood would be targeted. As soldiers gathered at their rally points, boys posted as lookouts would sprint back to warn their communities. For those harboring or aiding guerrillas, it was a race against time—a desperate scramble to hide food, supplies, or any trace of the resistance before the soldiers arrived.

Through the zonas, the Kempeitai also sought to root out guerrillas themselves. Sometimes they were searching for an unfamiliar face—a young man who couldn't convincingly explain why he was staying with a particular family. Other times, they simply rounded up all able-bodied men and hauled them off. Many of those taken never returned.

The Kempeitai were often assisted by Filipino collaborators. To most Filipinos, these men were the lowest form of life—even lower than the Japanese occupiers. Papa Emilio, whose refined upbringing meant he rarely used profanity, reserved his harshest words for them. Only a small percentage of Filipinos voluntarily aided the Japanese, but we remained constantly vigilant for this enemy among us—ready to sell out their countrymen for profit, revenge, or the promise of a better life.

Collaborators were rewarded for turning in guerrilla sympathizers, but they also profited from exposing smugglers and black marketeers. While most civilians endured hunger and malnutrition, collaborators lived lives of relative ease, shielded by their association with the enemy.

During the zonas, they served as interpreters and informants, pointing out alleged guerrillas or sympathizers within the neighborhoods. To conceal their identities, some wore *bayongs*—woven palm bags with tiny slits cut for their eyes. But even with their faces hidden, they were often easy to spot: huskier than their neighbors, whose bodies had grown thin from the deprivation of war.

I was twelve years old when I witnessed my first zona. It began at dawn, just as Mama Doray set about preparing breakfast with our meager rations. Paco, a neighborhood boy came running down the street yelling, "Zona, zona! The Japanese are coming!"

We could hear the rumble of trucks carrying the soldiers as they approached. As they jumped out of the back of the trucks, billows of dust formed as they assembled into a loose formation. Sharp whistles and orders shouted in Japanese cut through the morning air. I could see the look of fear on the faces of Papa Emilio and Mama Doray. My protectors, the ones who I had always counted on to shield me from harm were afraid, just as I was. It was an unsettling feeling.

The Kempeitai ordered everyone on our block out of their homes, the commands shouted in Japanese and Tagalog. Families spilled into the street, clutching their identification papers like lifelines. I held tightly to Mama Doray's trembling hand as we stepped outside. "Don't speak," she whispered, "and don't move unless I say." She tried to steady her voice, but the tremor betrayed her. The entire

Peñafiel clan huddled together in front of our house, and other families did the same—clusters of fear and uncertainty lining the road.

We were fearful for Papa Emilio and Joseling. Although this was our first zona, we had heard from other neighborhoods that the men in the household were always targeted. Papa Emilio was already in his sixties and Joseling had a permanently injured arm from an accident at work. Neither fit the profile of a guerrilla. Silently we prayed they would be spared.

A few houses up the street, the Flores family stood in a tight cluster. Even from a distance, I could see their eldest son, Pablo, sweating profusely, his perspiration glistening in the morning sun. He had returned only a month earlier, supposedly from visiting relatives in the province. That was the story the Flores family told. But rumors swirled—whispers that Pablo had joined the guerrillas. We knew better than to speak of it.

The Japanese, accompanied by their Filipino quislings, moved methodically down the block, stopping at each family to begin their questioning. They demanded identification papers and scrutinized every face. When they reached the Flores family, Pablo's mother insisted he had been helping at her cousin's farm. The Kempeitai officer didn't seem convinced. He barked a command, and moments later a man stepped forward, his face masked by a woven palm sack.

Even beneath the woven mask, I recognized the man by his build and clothing. In better times he had once sold vegetables at the market, known for his infectious smile and cheerful demeanor. Now, he was a shadow of that memory, a menacing version of his former self.

Slowly, he raised his arm and pointed at Pablo, saying something I couldn't make out. I held my breath as the soldiers grabbed Pablo and dragged him away. His mother screamed, begging them to let her son go, but the officer's face remained impassive.

Having apprehended their intended suspect, the Japanese returned to their trucks and departed as swiftly as they had arrived. We exhaled a collective sigh of relief. The Kempeitai hadn't reached our house and for now, Papa Emilio and Joseling were safe.

The same couldn't be said for poor Pablo. We learned later that the Japanese took him to a nearby garrison, set up on the grounds of a school they had commandeered. There were stories of anguished cries heard from behind its walls. No one knew exactly what he endured, whether he confessed or gave up his comrades. What we did know was this: the Japanese eventually returned Pablo's lifeless, broken body to his family. A grim warning to the rest of us.

We used to think our family was safe from the zonas. We weren't aiding the guerrillas, and neither Papa Emilio nor Joseling fit the profile of those typically rounded up. But we soon learned that safety was fragile—and that a neighbor with an axe to grind could turn a zona into a tool for retribution.

Such was the case with Mr. Ramos and Mr. Delarosa. Both were part of a group of neighborhood gamblers, a modest gathering of men who regularly played a small stakes, "friendly" game of cards. Mr. Ramos, known for his hot temper and poor sportsmanship, grew increasingly bitter over his losing streak to Mr. Delarosa, a mild-mannered man whose only offense was a run of good luck. Mr. Ramos, unconvinced that cheating wasn't involved, decided to do something about it.

One morning, the Japanese descended on our neighborhood with their usual clamor—trucks rumbling, boots pounding, orders shouted in clipped Japanese. This time, the Kempeitai and their Filipino lackeys were accompanied by a seemingly familiar man whose face was covered by a *bayong*. Even with the mask, everyone in the neighborhood knew it was Mr. Ramos. He pointed out Mr. Delarosa, who was immediately apprehended and dragged away, his frantic pleas proclaiming innocence falling on deaf ears.

Fortunately for Mr. Delarosa, it didn't take long for the Japanese to realize he had been falsely accused. Unfortunately, he still endured a brutal beating by the Kempeitai. Mr. Delarosa was summarily released and returned home, severely battered and bruised, but still alive.

But Mr. Ramos did not escape unscathed. A few days later, the Japanese returned. The officer in charge, furious at having been manipulated, ordered the apprehension of Mr. Ramos. He was hauled off kicking and screaming. Like Mr. Delarosa, Mr. Ramos was eventually released, but not before receiving a savage thrashing to teach him a lesson.

The zonas left scars on all of us. They were more than raids—they were brutal reminders of the power the Japanese held over our lives. Beyond the visible shows of force, the more insidious threat was how the zonas sowed fear and mistrust among neighbors, friends, even relatives. Once solid bonds could dissolve overnight, undone by suspicion. And perhaps most chilling of all was the slow erosion of life's value—a person could vanish in exchange for a few extra rations of rice or canned meat.

Yet in the quiet hours of the night, we found strength. Mama Doray, unwavering in her faith, would lead us in praying the Rosary, her voice steady as she added an extra prayer for the souls taken by the zonas. Though fear lingered—fear that the next raid might claim someone we loved—we clung to the fragile threads of our humanity. Through faith and prayer, we refused to let the darkness consume us entirely.

18 Seeing Dead People

The sight of dead people became commonplace during the war. It wasn't something that scared me; in fact, I found it intriguing. Oddly enough, the first time I saw a dead body was before the war.

One day, when I was eight, I waited outside school for Mama Doray to pick me up. My school was next to a church, and I could hear the sounds of a Mass in progress. This wasn't the usual time for the daily Masses.

"What's going on?" I asked a fellow student who was also waiting outside.

"It's a funeral," he replied.

I had never been to a funeral and was curious.

"Let's go check it out," I suggested, trying to convince some of the other kids to join me.

"No way! There's a dead person in there!" one of them exclaimed.

"So what? Don't you want to see what a dead person looks like?"

They all shook their heads.

"Okay then, I'll go myself," I declared.

"Alright," one of the kids said. "Let us know what you see."

Playing the role of a solo, intrepid explorer, I ventured into the church to investigate. This sort of wandering always seemed to get me into trouble. Mama Doray often told me to wait for her and not wander off, but my curiosity overruled my better judgment.

The church wasn't as full as it would have been for a Sunday Mass. A group of people had gathered near the altar, crowded around a large box—the casket. I couldn't make out who was inside, so I moved closer.

Lying in the casket was a young man, perhaps in his twenties. He looked peaceful, as though he were simply taking a nap. No one seemed to notice or mind as I approached, so I reached out and touched his hand, neatly folded across his chest. To my surprise, it didn't feel much different from the skin of a living person.

I stared at his face. He was handsome, and I wondered what had happened to him. Who was he? What kind of life had he lived? Around me, people were weeping, including an older couple nearby—perhaps his parents? They were grief-stricken. It was clear how much they missed him.

Just as I turned to head back to my classmates to report my findings, I saw Mama Doray. The anger on her face was unmistakable.

I approached her slowly, fully aware of what was coming next. As soon as I was within arm's reach, she grabbed me by the earlobe and led me out of the church.

"Didn't I tell you to wait for me outside?" she scolded.

All I could manage was a feeble, "Yes, Mama."

My classmates, watching the scene unfold, giggled in hushed tones.

It was embarrassing, but it was worth it—I had seen my first dead person. Four years would pass before I saw the next one.

By 1943, the war had been raging for nearly two years. Most of the kids in our neighborhood had grown up fast, as children often do in wartime. Mama Doray wasn't as strict about who I hung out with or how long I stayed outside. School bells and familiar routines had disappeared—survival was now the priority, and everyone had a role to play. I was part of a small group of neighborhood kids who went on foraging missions. For us, it was a mix of necessity and adventure, driven by hunger and the strange freedom that chaos brought.

We knew which trees grew guavas or star apples and which households had banana plants half-hidden in their yards. We knew every creek, every patch of vegetation where anything remotely edible might be found. I learned to sneak silently through gaps in fences, my eyes sharp for anything that looked nourishing, but more often than not, we came away with little. That day, however, we stumbled on something else entirely.

I'll never forget the moment I saw him—half-submerged in the creek that ran through a lightly wooded area. A Japanese soldier lay still, his arms sprawled awkwardly as though he'd been dropped from the sky. We froze, caught in a web of silence, each of us staring at this figure who had always been a distant threat, now suddenly within reach.

His uniform was soaked and clung tightly to his body, his hand stretched into the shallow water as though he'd been trying to grasp something. I tilted my head, trying to see his face from different angles, noticing how the sunlight reflected off his still, waxy skin. His helmet was gone, likely swept away by the creek. There was no blood on his uniform, no visible injuries. Had he drowned? Slipped on a rock?

In my mind, I began piecing together his final moments, like a detective constructing a theory in a mystery novel. I imagined him slipping on a slick stone, hitting his head as he fell, and ultimately drowning in the shallow water. The scene felt surreal, but not frightening.

"He must have been hungry when he died," I remarked.

"How do you know that?" one of the other kids asked.

"Because his eyes are open," I replied confidently. "Everyone knows that."

They nodded in agreement, though I had no idea whether it was true.

We didn't linger; we knew that if Japanese soldiers found us near their fallen comrade, the consequences would be dire. As we slipped away, I wondered what Mama Doray would say if she saw me standing over a dead soldier. I could imagine her horrified gasp, maybe even a firm squeeze of my earlobe for good measure.

Not long after, as I was walking to a neighbor's house to fetch some *camote* (sweet potato) leaves, I saw another body. This time the corpse was slumped in a drainage ditch off to the side of the path. He was lying face down, his back covered in dirt and leaves. I paused, studying him. This man felt different from the soldier; he seemed familiar somehow. His bare feet were caked with mud, his clothes torn in places. He reminded me of someone's uncle—the kind of man who might sell fish at the market or pull a cart filled with firewood.

I crouched to get a better look, my mind swirling with questions. Who was he? What had happened to him? Was he a fighter, or just someone caught in the wrong place at the wrong time? My imagination filled in the blanks: maybe he had been picked up by the Japanese for aiding the guerrillas, his lifeless body dumped by the side of the road after succumbing to torture.

Just as I was lost in thought, the neighbor, *Señora* Santos, appeared, her voice sharp with concern. "*Ay, niña*, don't stand there!" she said, grabbing my arm. Seeing the man in the ditch, her face had turned pale. She quickly handed me a bundle of camote leaves. "Go now, run home, and don't stop!"

Her voice trembled as though even looking at the man could bring misfortune to her door. She hurried me away, gripping my shoulder tightly until I was a safe distance from the ditch.

As soon as I got home, I told Mama Doray about the dead man by the side of the road. She made the sign of the cross and uttered a brief, silent prayer. She then warned me not to wander too far or into any unfamiliar places. I nodded, though I knew it was a promise I would inevitably break.

As the conflict persisted, the images of the dead lingered in my mind. They weren't haunting or supernatural—they were stark reminders of how fragile life had become. A person could die in the middle of a quiet neighborhood or along a familiar path. Strangely, I wasn't afraid of this reality. Perhaps I had already accepted it as part of my world.

19 Matinee At The Ideal

Mama and Papa were arguing. I couldn't hear what they were arguing about, but Mama Doray seemed to be very upset with Papa Emilio. My adoptive parents didn't have a lot of arguments, so on the few occasions that it happened I knew it was about something serious. Because their arguments were such a rare event, hearing them raise their voices at each other was very distressing. This is usually the case when children see their parents arguing. But this particular morning I wasn't as bothered by their arguing because I was going to the cinema to watch a movie with Papa Emilio!

Earlier that morning Papa greeted me with a surprise announcement, "Ging, we are going to watch a movie this afternoon at the Ideal Theater." Actually, it was more of a matter-of-fact statement than a surprise announcement. Papa didn't seem to be as excited about going to the movies as I was. Even before the war, a trip to the cinema was a treat in the Peñafiel household. The fact that we would be watching a movie in the midst of this war made it even more exciting.

Before the war, Manila was home to several top-notch movie theaters, such as the Ideal, Capitol, Lyric, Bellevue, Radio, State, and Life. Many of these cinemas were grand structures, designed by renowned Filipino architects in classic Art Deco style with modern conveniences such as plush seating and air conditioning. Throughout the late 1930's and continuing until the early 1940's, these movie houses were screening the latest Hollywood box office hits, as well as films locally produced by Sampaguita Pictures and LVN Studios.

It was during those years that Mama Doray would occasionally treat me to a movie featuring my favorite actress: Shirley Temple. Like many of her fans, I was captivated by this spunky little girl with the curly hair and dimples. Watching Shirley Temple's adventures play out on the big screen, I was immersed in a make-believe world where the heroine was a child, not much older than I was at the time. Like other girls my age, I wanted to be like Shirley Temple, or more specifically, like the characters she played on the big screen.

But that was before the war, before the Japanese arrived in the Philippines. During the occupation, the Japanese confiscated most of the movies made in the US and Europe, replacing them with propaganda films and locally produced films that were sanctioned by the Japanese. However, a few theaters managed to hold on to a limited stock of American films, mostly westerns and comedies, and would play them over and over again.

I was hoping that the Ideal theater would be playing an American film that afternoon, perhaps one featuring Shirley Temple. I didn't even care if it was a movie I had seen before. Just to see her familiar face again would be enough to lift my spirits amidst the bleakness of my wartime existence.

After a while I couldn't hear Mama and Papa arguing any more so I took that as my cue to venture out in the living room. Papa Emilio was there alone, a glum look on his face. Whatever he and Mama Doray were arguing about obviously affected him, but I was sure an afternoon at the cinema would help cheer him up.

I was pleasantly surprised to find out we would be catching a taxi cab to the movie theater. Before the war we would often ride a taxi whenever we went into town. However, after the Japanese took over the country, transportation became limited and we seldom ventured out, let alone in a taxi.

During the taxi ride through town, Papa remained eerily silent, which was so unlike him. Whenever I traveled with Papa Emilio, he would always point out a particular building, statue, or other landmark and explain its historical significance or share an interesting fact about it. This afternoon there was none of that. Instead, Papa stared out into the distance, his mind preoccupied by something else.

As I settled in for the ride to the theater, I tried not to let Papa's sullen mood bring me down too. After all, I was going to see a movie in the middle of the war! The closer to the theater, the more excited I became about seeing the movie. The other kids in the neighborhood would be so jealous when they heard that I saw a movie at the Ideal theater.

As we approached the Ideal, I could see in the distance that there were a few people waiting outside. To me that was a good sign; the movie had not started yet. Maybe we would have enough time to get some popcorn or candy. I was sure I could convince Papa Emilio that I was deserving of a treat. The closer we got to the theater, the more clearly I could see the people waiting out front. I leaned closer to the window. To my shock, I realized that the people waiting outside the theater were no ordinary movie goers – they were Japanese soldiers!

I was sure that Papa also noticed the Japanese soldiers and that he would tell the taxi driver to continue on and bring us back home. As much as I wanted to watch a movie, being in the same theater as the enemy was not worth the risk. Although I had not personally witnessed atrocities committed by the occupying Japanese Army, I had heard the stories, told in hushed voices, between the grown ups. Stories of people being severely beaten for violating curfew. Stories of neighbors whisked away in the middle of the night, never to be seen or heard from again. Stories of suspected guerilla collaborators publicly beheaded. It was most certainly best to avoid any encounters or interaction with the Japanese.

I sat back in the seat, a little disappointed that we wouldn't be watching a movie, but I knew it was for the best. Perhaps Papa would have the cab driver take us some place for ice cream to make it up to me. I wondered if there were still shops serving ice cream during the war. I guess it didn't really matter. What mattered was that we were getting out of harm's way.

Then something totally unexpected happened. The taxi stopped in front of the theater! Maybe Papa hadn't noticed the Japanese soldiers? But they were right there, plain as day! How could he not see them? Maybe he was in shock? I knew he would snap out of it any moment and tell the driver to continue on. But he didn't. Instead he handed the driver the fare, opened the door and stepped out of the cab. He then motioned for me to get out as well.

I slowly slid across the back seat and exited the taxi, reaching out to take Papa's outstretched hand. I wanted to tell Papa that it was okay, I didn't really want to watch a movie today. That it wasn't too late to get back into the cab and leave. But now I was in a state of shock, rendered speechless.

Since Papa seemed determined to take me to the theater, perhaps the best thing was for us to make a beeline for the entrance and hope the Japanese soldiers wouldn't notice us. Surely an older Filipino man and her young daughter posed no threat to the Imperial Army. Instinctively I started moving in that direction, confident that Papa would follow suit. Then something totally unexpected happened again. Papa headed straight for the Japanese soldiers!

I was in a stupor, confused by what was happening. I wanted to break free from Papa's hand and run away. But where would I go? Maybe I could get back to the cab, if it was still there. But I couldn't leave Papa. Maybe he would come to his senses and we could both run back to the taxi. But Papa didn't come to his senses – we just both kept walking towards the soldiers.

As we approached the Japanese soldiers, I got a clearer look at them. There were three of them, each carrying a gun. This was the closest I had ever been to a Japanese soldier. From a distance, they had always seemed frightening enough, but standing directly in front of them, they were even more intimidating. They were tall, perhaps taller than Papa Emilio. Their uniforms were immaculate—clean and meticulously pressed.

We stopped a few feet away, and Papa bowed deeply, a gesture of reverence and submission to the occupiers. The soldier in the middle gave a subtle nod in response. He seemed to be the leader, likely an officer. I knew I had to show respect as well. Trembling with fear, I lowered my head and cautiously bowed.

As I raised my head, I thought I caught a faint smile on the officer's face. Was I imagining it? Or was it more of a sneer?

Then, something completely unexpected happened. The officer reached into his uniform coat pocket and pulled out an object. Extending his hand, he offered it to me. It was a candy stick—something I hadn't seen since before the war. It was swirled with yellow and white, like a tiny work of art. For a moment, I was mesmerized, almost forgetting who was holding it.

I looked up at Papa. He nodded silently, giving me permission to accept the gift. Slowly, I reached out and took the candy stick from the officer's hand. My fingers brushed against his glove, and I felt a chill. Hesitantly, I glanced up at him again, and there it was—another faint smile, or so I thought.

The officer gestured toward the theater entrance, and one of the soldiers began walking in that direction. Papa and I followed closely, with the officer and the remaining soldier trailing behind us. We passed through the empty lobby and entered the dimly lit theater. The only light came from the flickering images on the screen, casting eerie shadows across the rows of seats.

The lead soldier stopped about five rows from the front and gestured for us to sit to the right of the center aisle. Papa went in first, settling a few seats from the aisle. Still clutching his hand with my right and holding the candy stick in my left, I sat down beside him.

I glanced over my shoulder to see where the soldiers had gone. The one who had led us down the aisle was nowhere to be seen. Only the officer and the other soldier remained. The officer handed his belt and holstered pistol to the soldier, then paused as if preparing to sit. I silently prayed he would choose a seat far away from us—across the aisle, maybe even in another row.

But my worst fear came true. To my horror, the officer entered our row and took the seat right next to me.

My body froze. I gripped Papa's hand tighter, my heart pounding in my chest. I faced the screen, my eyes wide, but I couldn't focus on the movie. The officer, on the other hand, seemed relaxed. Occasionally, he tapped my arm and said something in Japanese, his tone light, as though trying to engage me. At times, he even laughed softly, seemingly amused by the film. I didn't dare look at him, too consumed by fear to move or respond.

I wished desperately for the movie to end, for the lights to come back on so we could leave. But time seemed to stretch endlessly. Then, out of the corner of my eye, I noticed the officer lean toward Papa. They exchanged a few words in English, but I was too dazed to catch their meaning.

What happened next sent a fresh wave of terror through me. The officer began tapping his thighs with both hands, gesturing for me to sit on his lap. My stomach dropped. The thought alone was unbearable. I turned to Papa, my eyes pleading for him to say no. But his face was somber, his expression pained. Slowly, he nodded.

Reluctantly, I obeyed. My legs felt like lead as I stood up and moved toward the officer. My hands trembled as I climbed onto his lap. I felt utterly powerless, consumed by confusion and fear, wishing for it all to end.

Afraid to make any movement, I sat rigidly on the officer's lap. As before, he continued speaking to me in Japanese while the movie played. His demeanor was calm, and although I couldn't understand his words, they didn't seem menacing or threatening. Yet, I was terrified beyond belief. What had started as a happy day for me had spiraled into a nightmare. What would happen next? Would we be apprehended and taken to a prison camp, never to see our family again? The fear of the unknown consumed me.

After what felt like an eternity, the movie finally ended. The lights came on, and the Japanese officer stood, gently lifting me off his lap and placing me beside Papa. Without a word, he gestured toward the exit. Papa and I followed him to the lobby, where we paused briefly to exchange farewells.

The soldier accompanying the officer handed him his belt and holster. The officer held up a hand, signaling a brief pause. Reaching into his pocket, he pulled out a photograph of a woman and a girl dressed in traditional Japanese attire. He crouched to my level, his eyes meeting mine. Showing me the photograph, he pointed to the girl, then to me, and said in English, "Same."

I looked up at his face and saw tears welling in his eyes. His expression was unmistakable—a sorrow I recognized. It was the same look I had seen on Papa Emilio's face months earlier when he said goodbye to his daughter Nena for the last time, on the day she passed away from pneumonia.

The officer stood upright, adjusted his jacket, and fastened his belt and holster. Papa faced him and gave a deep bow. The officer returned a nod, his face solemn.

The same taxi from earlier was waiting for us. We climbed in and began the slow journey home. As we pulled away, I turned to look back, catching a final glimpse of the Japanese officer standing motionless, watching as our taxi disappeared down the street. Papa and I rode the rest of the way in silence.

20 Weight Of Hunger

By 1944, living conditions in the Philippines had gone from bad to worse. Hunger gnawed at us like a persistent rat. Manila—once a bustling city, a vibrant mix of Spanish colonial charm and American influence—now bore the scars of occupation. Storefronts were shuttered, and the streets echoed with the trudge of weary souls, all searching for food, a glimmer of hope, or perhaps both.

Before the Japanese arrived, my days were marked by the sweet aroma of freshly baked pandesal from the bakery down the street, the inviting scent of grilled meat skewers from the corner vendor, and the comforting warmth of chicken adobo simmering in Mama Doray's kitchen. But those days had faded into distant memory.

Food had become scarce and astronomically expensive, and what little we could obtain was often of poor quality—old, pest-ridden, or spoiled. The worst of it was *sisid* rice. In Tagalog, sisid means "dive," a direct reference to how it was recovered.

At the outset of the war, Japanese bombers sank several merchant ships in Manila Bay. As food supplies dwindled, desperate residents dove to the sea floor to retrieve sacks of rice trapped inside the twisted hulls of those wrecked vessels. It was punishing, perilous work—a testament to the lengths Filipinos would go to feed their families.

The rice, buried in silt and saltwater for over a year, was rancid at best. It had to be dried in the sun for days, and even then, it was barely edible. To make it tolerable, the rice was boiled to remove the stench, then fried with garlic and spices, hoping to mask the flavor. But the smell lingered. We told ourselves it was better than nothing. Even so, hunger couldn't quiet the revulsion. We held our breath when we ate it.

Our family, like so many others, lived hand to mouth. Mama Doray stretched what little we had with camote or mixed it with cornmeal. On the rare occasions we had fish or meat, she seasoned it sparingly, rationing salt and soy sauce as if they were gold dust. We foraged for whatever the land could offer—*kangkong* (water spinach) by the riverbanks, papaya leaves, even the tough cassava roots that took forever to boil. My stomach learned to quiet its protests, but my mind never stopped calculating how many meals we could eke out of our dwindling supplies.

Hunger taught us to see value in everything. We saved every scrap, dried fish bones for broth, and even boiled banana peels when times grew desperate. We grew lean but resourceful, and in that forced ingenuity, I learned lessons that shaped me far beyond those harrowing years.

I felt a particular ache for Bobby, Carlota's baby. At barely a year old, he was fragile and helpless, his cries piercing through the night—a reminder of the sustenance we couldn't provide. Milk had become nearly impossible to acquire. Instead, we made do with rice water, sweetened with the tiniest sprinkle of sugar, if we could find any. I watched as his once-plump cheeks hollowed out and his eyes grew too large for his face. His frailty was a painful reminder of how precarious our survival had become.

Amidst this chaos and scarcity, the black market rose like a shadowy savior. Families like ours turned to bartering prized possessions for food smuggled in from the provinces. It started small—family jewelry traded for sacks of rice or canned goods. As those items dwindled, we bartered pieces of furniture, including our piano. All of the Peñafiel girls took lessons on that piano. I had just begun mine before the war. That piece of family tradition was now gone, hauled away to the province in exchange for a few cans of food.

When the hunger became too much to bear, I would wander to Millie's house. Millie was a neighborhood friend who was a year younger than me. Her father worked as a cook for the Japanese garrison, which gave her family access to leftovers and other food items the Japanese soldiers intended to discard. For Millie's family, the constant pressure of starvation was less severe; they had their own kind of survival plan.

In Millie's house, there was always the lilt of another language—a rhythm and melody I recognized but didn't speak. Millie's family spoke Chabacano, a creole language that is a blend of Spanish and local Philippine dialects, most notably Tagalog and Cebuano.

Each evening, I timed my "visits" carefully, knowing when Millie's father would come home. I'd linger outside their house, too embarrassed to venture past the porch but always hoping for the smell of cooked rice or soup to drift out.

Millie's mother was kind and never chased me away, but chose rather to share her family's meager rations. She'd call out to Millie in Chabacano, "*¿Onde está tu amiga?*"—"Where is your friend?"

"*Está aquí,*" she'd reply, letting her mother know I was outside waiting.

When I came around, Millie's mother always prepared an extra meal—a small bowl of rice and a piece of meat, usually fish or chicken. She'd hand it to Millie, who brought it out to me on the porch.

The first time she did this, I felt a pang of guilt so sharp I almost handed the food back. I thought of my adoptive family at the Peñafiel home, especially the younger ones, their eyes growing more sunken with each passing day. But I was too famished to refuse. I wolfed down the food before the taste could even register, ashamed of how desperately I devoured it.

Each time I finished, I told myself it was only a small

portion—barely enough for one person, much less a family. Besides, my family would never have known. I had nothing to bring home; my hands were empty, and the shame was mine alone to bear. Still, the guilt crept in, gnawing at me like a second hunger. I wanted to be strong enough to save half, to share even a spoonful, but each bite tasted like survival—something I couldn't let slip away.

The visits to Millie's house became a quiet ritual. I learned not to say much, to simply take my place on the porch as if it were the most natural thing in the world. Sometimes Millie would sit beside me, sharing stories or small jokes that made me forget, for a moment, that we were living through something relentless and cruel. There, with her quiet companionship and a small bowl of rice, I could pretend I was just a girl sitting with her friend—not a scavenger stealing moments of relief from an enemy intent on starving us out.

The war continued without mercy, yet somehow we endured. We found ways to forage, to trade, to stretch what little we had. I even found my own way to survive, selfish as it was. Looking back, it's strange to think how those hurried, hidden bites could hold so much—how they felt like the thin line between survival and defeat.

21 Lola Sima

Lola Sima, Mama Doray's mother, was a small woman, her back slightly hunched from years of domestic labor in the homes of wealthy Spanish families. As slight and frail as she appeared, she held the strength of a mountain in my eyes. Her hands were gnarled and calloused from decades of scrubbing floors, doing laundry, and mending clothes, yet I watched those same hands pound rice into flour, weave delicate baskets, and crochet lace. She always seemed to have the energy to keep herself busy.

I called her Lola, even though she wasn't my biological grandmother. Mama Caring's mother had passed away before I was born, and my father's mother, Lola Julia, was distant and cold. To me, Lola Sima was my true grandmother.

Lola Sima was not a woman of many words, but her silences never felt empty. She spoke through her hands—hands that braided my hair, lifted me onto her lap when I was sick, and gently caressed my face when I was upset. That last gesture became familiar, as I often found myself in trouble.

As a child, I was spirited, and my impulsiveness was often my downfall. Whether it was fidgeting around in church, playing outside instead of finishing my chores, or knocking over a vase while running around the house, I always seemed to be at the center of some mishap. Mama Doray was quick to scold me when these incidents occurred. Her sharp voice and firm hand—though never cruel—always sent me running whenever I knew I had done something wrong.

And when that happened, there was only one place I could go—straight to Lola Sima.

I would find her in the kitchen, where she always seemed to be, stirring a pot or kneading dough for pandesal. At the first sight of her, my fear would dissolve into sobs. Tears would stream down my face, and my small hands would grab at the hem of her skirt, hiding my face in the soft fabric as I cried out my shame. I didn't have to say a word—Lola knew. She always knew.

Lola Sima would take a momentary pause from cooking and reach down, her worn, weathered hand cupping the back of my head, gently pulling me closer. "Now, now," she would whisper, her voice as calm as the ocean after a storm. "What's wrong my little one?"

Through hiccups and sniffling, I would confess my misdeeds. Sometimes it was small things—a broken plate, a missing curio. Other times, it was something bigger, like the time I knocked over an entire tray of chorizo that Mama Doray had spent the day preparing. No matter the gravity of my mistake, Lola's response was always the same. She never raised her voice. Instead, she would listen quietly, nodding as I stammered through my explanations.

When I was done, she would gently wipe my face with the edge of her apron. "It's okay, just apologize to your Mama," she'd say softly, reminding me that there were consequences for my actions. But she didn't lecture me. Instead, she would guide me back to my feet, sending me on my way with a light pat on my back, her hands lingering just long enough to make me feel safe again.

Lola Sima spoiled me in her own way, a kindness I sometimes learned to take advantage of. Before the war, Papa Emilio would often bring home a sack of boiled peanuts for the family. The peanuts would be divided equally into portions for each person. After quickly devouring mine, I wanted more. So, in a moment of childish greed, I would go to Lola Sima and tell her a little lie. "Lola," I said, "I didn't get any peanuts. Can I have some of yours?"

Lola looked at me with those deep, knowing eyes. Of course, she knew I was fibbing, but she didn't scold me. Instead, with a soft smile, she reached into her pouch and shared her peanuts with me.

"Here, anak," she said in a gentle voice. "Since you didn't get any," she added with a knowing wink. "Just don't tell anyone."

As much as I loved the special treatment from Lola Sima, I could tell that Mama Doray disapproved and the two of them would often argue about it.

"Why do you baby her so much?" Mama Doray would ask, scolding Lola Sima.

"She's just a little girl, let her enjoy her childhood."

"I don't remember you being that lenient with me as a child," Mama Doray responded.

Lola Sima would chuckle, "Those were different times. Besides, a grandmother is supposed to spoil her grandchild."

Aside from her lax treatment of me, there was something else that Mama Doray resented about her mother—a grievance it seemed she could never forgive her for. It was the fact that Lola Sima held her back from continuing her education when she was younger.

"A woman doesn't need much schooling beyond 6th grade. She only needs to know how to read and do simple math. If you're a housekeeper you don't need much more than that!" declared Lola Sima.

"But I want to be more than a housekeeper," Mama Doray would protest. "I want to be a teacher or maybe a nurse."

"Bah!" Lola Sima would scoff. "Who's filling your head with that nonsense? Eventually you will get married and raise a family. You don't need to get an education and work."

Mama Doray felt it was no use arguing with her mother. She was from a different era, when a woman's place was in the home. Mama Doray couldn't do anything to change her destiny. But when she had children of her own, she made sure they got an education, and encouraged them to pursue a career, something more than being a laborer or housewife.

Even though it was all past history, Mama Doray would often bring it up during their frequent arguments. It was during these times that Lola Sima would threaten to leave and stay with some other relative.

I would see her packing a small valise with some of her belongings and would ask her where she's going.

"Your Mama doesn't want me here anymore, so I'm leaving," she'd respond.

"Can I go with you Lola?" I'd ask.

"Not now, anak, but maybe I'll send for you later."

Mama Doray and I knew she was bluffing because she would eventually unpack her bag and stay home. But this scene played out whenever they quarreled.

As the war persisted, so did the scarcity of food. Hunger became a constant companion, and malnutrition took its toll on everyone, especially the elderly and the frail. Lola Sima was no exception. Around this time, the strife between them stopped. Maybe it was because they were both in a weakened state. Or maybe Mama Doray realized that, in the midst of the war, life was too short to hold grudges. Whatever the reason, the squabbles between Lola and Mama ended.

Understanding the severity of the situation, Lola Sima insisted on having smaller portions during meals.

"I'm old anyway," she would say, her voice calm and resolute. "I don't have much time left on this Earth. It's better that my food goes to the younger ones."

Her selflessness, though admirable, came at a price. Day by day, her strength waned, and eventually, she became too weak to leave her bed.

I remember sitting by her bedside, holding her hand in mine as she took her final breaths. Those hands, once so strong and capable, had become frail and thin, their veins standing out like rivers on a worn map. Yet, even in her last moments, her grip remained steady.

She gave my hand one final squeeze—a gesture of reassurance, as if to say, *"It's okay, anak. I'm still with you."*

When she passed, I cried harder than I ever had before. It felt as though the very foundation of my world had crumbled. Lola Sima had been my anchor, a shelter during my times of anguish. And even though we weren't related by blood, to Lola Sima I was the granddaughter who ran to her for comfort, wisdom, and love. Her death left a gaping hole in my heart, one I didn't know how to fill.

After she was gone, the emptiness became unbearable. I would catch myself searching for her in the kitchen, half-expecting to find her there, her hands busy stirring a pot of soup or mending a tear in my dress. Each time I realized she wasn't there, the tears would come again.

But beyond the grief, I couldn't shake the guilt—guilt for not sharing the food from Millie's family. If I had brought even a few spoonfuls for Lola, perhaps she would still be alive. If I hadn't been so selfish, maybe she would have survived.

I carried that feeling of remorse for days—until I had a dream.

In the dream, Lola Sima came to me. She wasn't frail or fading; she was the strong, energetic woman I remembered from my younger days. Dressed in white, her face radiated a serene glow. As soon as I saw her, I ran to her, and she welcomed me with a warm, comforting embrace.

"Don't be sad, my child. I am in a beautiful place, and it was my time to go," she said.

"But I want to be with you, Lola. Can I come with you?"

"It's not your time yet, my child. But don't worry—we'll see each other again one day."

She gently cupped my face in her hands and smiled—a beautiful, peaceful smile. And then, she was gone.

I awoke with a profound sense of tranquility. The war still raged around us, and the future remained uncertain, but somehow I knew everything would be okay.

Even though Lola Sima was gone, I carried her with me. My heart still ached at her loss, but through her message in that dream, I knew I would always find the strength to persevere—even when things felt impossible.

22 Turning Tide

In the summer of 1944, whispered chatter among the adults was that the Americans were winning the war and that they would soon return. Half a world away, we heard that Allied forces had landed on a beach in Normandy, France, beating the Germans into retreat. We all dreamed of the day the US military would land on our shores too, liberating us from the Japanese. Our parents told us not to talk about it—to keep our heads down and not let on what we knew—but how could we not hope? We caught scraps of conversation in our neighborhood: mothers murmuring to each other while washing clothes, men speaking in hushed voices behind drawn curtains after curfew. Even the parish priest hinted at it in his sermon, urging us to pray for deliverance.

The whispers took on new urgency in late October 1944. Early one morning, one of Papa Emilio's friends, Señor Lim, came to our house, his face flushed with excitement.

"They're here," he said in a loud whisper, as if the Japanese might be standing outside. "The Americans have landed in Leyte!"

Papa Emilio let out a surprised gasp. Mama Doray began to sob softly, tears of joy and relief streaming down her face. Papa pressed Señor Lim for more details. On October 20, 1944, the US military mounted an amphibious assault on the island of Leyte. They secured the beachhead, and troops—led by General Douglas MacArthur himself—waded ashore.

"General MacArthur kept his promise! He returned to liberate us!" Señor Lim exclaimed.

The news spread like wildfire from house to house, each retelling filling the streets of our San Juan neighborhood with a rare, cautious hope. We could hardly believe it—the thought of American forces landing on our soil again after all this time felt like a dream.

In the streets, everyone spoke of Leyte. Neighbors exchanged snippets of information they'd heard from others, all of us piecing together the story of MacArthur's return like a patchwork quilt of hope. We learned of massive ships in Leyte Gulf, of American planes filling the skies, of fierce battles against the Japanese who clung to the islands tenaciously. It was hard to imagine the fighting that was taking place so far from the familiar streets of San Juan, but knowing the Americans were back—fighting their way through our islands to reach us—filled us with a renewed strength.

But in the weeks that followed, the war no longer felt far away. The sound of planes overhead became part of our days. Aerial battles, which had been rare before, now erupted almost daily. We didn't fully understand the danger; we only knew that the sky had come alive with movement and noise. To us children, it was both terrifying and wondrous—a kind of forbidden spectacle that broke the monotony of fear and hunger.

We used to climb the roof of a nearby building whenever we heard the rumbling engines approaching. Lack of food made us brave—or maybe just foolish—and watching the dogfights became our strange kind of pastime. From up there, the air felt closer, louder. We could see the silver American planes marked with stars and the Japanese Zeroes with their red suns, circling each other like birds of prey. When the guns crackled, we ducked behind tin sheets, oblivious to the danger. Sometimes one of the planes went down, a long streak of smoke unraveling behind it. If it was a Japanese plane, we cheered. If it was an American plane, we remained still, holding a reverent moment of silence.

By the end of 1944, the battles came nearly every day. We watched from wherever we could get a good view—from rooftops, from open fields, from palm groves. I remember crouching beneath the trees once, pretending the fronds could shield me. The Japanese Zeroes were fast, darting and vicious; the American P-38s, with their distinct twin bodies, looked like machines sent to punish the enemy. The warplanes squared off and, in an instant, the staccato of machine gun fire erupted across the sky. They chased each other with weapons blazing—a deadly game of tag in midair. And just as quickly as it began, the skirmish was over. That day, the Americans emerged as the victors, and for a moment, hope felt real.

Then came January 1945. The Americans had landed on Luzon, and we could see their planes bombing the Japanese bases beyond the city. The sky thundered with noise, the earth trembled, and smoke coiled upward like a mythical dark serpent. As the fight edged closer to our city, liberation became more tangible; freedom felt almost within our reach.

But it would be weeks before we learned what that fight would cost—before the liberation we longed for turned Manila into a battlefield.

23 "V" For Victory

With each new report, our spirits lifted, and I dared to imagine what it would be like when the Americans finally reached our neighborhood. Sometimes, my friends and I walked to the edge of San Juan, gazing down the road as if any day now we'd see trucks carrying American soldiers, their engines rumbling with the promise of freedom. We dreamed out loud, whispering plans for the future, picturing what our city would look like once the Japanese were gone. More and more, it felt like our nightmare might soon end.

But the Japanese soldiers seemed to sense it, too. Their eyes grew darker, their voices sharper. Patrols in the streets increased; they searched houses more often, bursting in without warning, hunting for anything suspicious. They were afraid, I realized—just as we were—though their fear made them cruel. Yet with the Americans so close, my own fear changed. It no longer kept me frozen or silent. It carried a strange strength, because for the first time in years, I was sure the war would end. And now, I could almost see that ending on the horizon.

As the weeks passed, whispers turned into quiet cheers that spread throughout San Juan and beyond. After landing at Lingayen Gulf on January 6, 1945, the Americans moved swiftly across Luzon, pushing southward in a race to retake Manila. Through the grapevine, we heard of town after town being liberated. Each city and province that returned to Filipino hands was like a heartbeat—steady, hopeful—a rhythm pulsing through our veins, reviving our spirits.

Each victory gave us new hope, and we clung to every scrap of news. In late January, Señor Lim stopped by our house with word that the Americans were nearing Manila. "It won't be long now," he told us, his face alight with excitement and tears. Papa Emilio embraced him, grateful for the hopeful news. Mama Doray made the sign of the cross—a silent prayer of thanks. Every rumor, every whisper of progress, felt like a promise—a promise that soon, we would be free.

In early February 1945, there was a sudden turn of events. Millie's father said that the soldiers at the local garrison had packed up their trucks and left. Soon, others in our neighborhood reported the same thing—the Japanese army was gone. To our astonishment, their departure was quickly followed by the arrival of the Americans.

When the first convoys rolled into San Juan, the whole city seemed to awaken. After years of fear and silence, people poured into the streets as if a dam had broken, all that sorrow and waiting bursting out as joy. It was a sight unlike anything I had ever seen—soldiers in olive drab uniforms, dusty and grinning, perched atop their trucks and tanks. Their faces were tired but shining as they looked out over the crowds of Filipinos cheering their arrival.

I ran outside with my friends, swept up in the rush of people. The air crackled with excitement. We waved with everything we had, shouting *"Mabuhay!"* and *"Salamat!"* until our voices were hoarse. People threw flowers at the convoys, showering the troops with garlands they had woven that very morning. Some of the men reached down from the trucks, clasping the hands raised toward them. They smiled as if they already knew us—as if we had been waiting for each other all along.

A group of us kids pushed to the front of the crowd, raising our hands high, forming "V" for victory with our fingers. It felt like a new language, a symbol for the hope, resilience, and strength that carried us through the long years of occupation. The soldiers smiled back, many of them lifting their own fingers in a "V" to match ours. I felt tears welling up as I looked up at them. Their faces were unfamiliar, yet I felt a quiet kinship with these strangers—our liberators.

Everywhere, people cheered, sang, and danced, their faces shining with joy and relief. Men and women, young and old, rushed out to hug the soldiers, laughing through their tears as they thanked them in broken English. The soldiers were genuinely touched by the welcome, their eyes widening at the warmth and gratitude they saw in every face. For the first time in years, we felt alive again, our streets filled with happiness instead of fear.

The celebratory atmosphere only lasted for a few hours, after which we received a dose of reality from the American soldiers. The Japanese had not fully abandoned the area, but rather regrouped in Manila's city center and other strategic points. They intended to make a last stand against the liberating US and Filipino forces, which meant that the fighting was far from over.

For now, we felt safe, knowing the occupiers were gone from our neighborhood and American soldiers were patrolling the area. But there was an uneasy feeling that the tide of war could change. After all, the Japanese had beaten the Americans before. Could it happen again? The feelings of doubt were deepened as the sounds of fierce combat erupted in the distance. Allied troops converged on Manila as they fought to retake it from the Japanese. The city center was only a few miles away from San Juan, a grim reminder that we were dangerously close to the fighting.

Manila became a battlefield overnight, and every street, every building, felt the weight of it. The Japanese dug in fiercely, refusing to surrender even as the Americans closed in. They were desperate, and their desperation was deadly. Our once-peaceful streets were turned into war zones, littered with rubble and scorched by fire. Homes were destroyed by bombs and artillery shells, and each new blast seemed to bring another building to the ground. The air reeked of smoke and burning wood, of metal and earth torn apart. In the distance, we could see the flames from the carnage; orange and red, they lit up the night like a second sun.

The Japanese held nothing back, and in their desperation, they became crueler than ever. Realizing they would not survive the Allied offensive, Japanese troops descended into a vicious rampage of burning, butchering, and plundering. They turned their wrath on innocent civilians, slaughtering entire families and laying waste to everything in their path. Stories trickled in from survivors who escaped the besieged capital, stories of the atrocities committed by the Japanese army. Stories that still haunt my dreams.

Finally, after weeks of fierce fighting, we heard the news that American and Filipino soldiers had crushed the last remnants of enemy resistance. On March 4, 1945, Manila was officially liberated. But the victory came at a heavy cost. Our city lay in ruins, the familiar sights of my childhood buried beneath ash and rubble. Entire neighborhoods had been destroyed. Plaza Lawton, once a bustling hub for the tranvia, was unrecognizable. The grand Manila Post Office was shattered, its marble pillars reduced to rubble. Intramuros, where I spent Sunday afternoons with Papa Emilio, lay broken, scarred by artillery. The city I loved, rich with history and childhood memories, had become a ghost of itself.

Yet, amid the devastation, there was a strange sense of peace. The Japanese were gone. The Americans had retaken Manila. And for the first time in years, we could step outside without fear and without the shadow of war pressing down on us. We were exhausted, but we were free.

The city was shattered, but its spirit—our spirit—remained unbroken. I knew that Manila would rise again. The scars left on the city were deep, and they would remain for years to come, a reminder of all that we had suffered. But they would also remind us of our strength—the resilience that carried us through the darkest days. I knew that, somehow, we would endure.

24 A GI's Warning

The euphoria of liberation was brief. After days and nights of jubilant street celebrations, a sobering truth settled in: the war was over for us, but the harder task lay ahead—rebuilding our lives, our homes, and our country.

The San Juan district survived the war relatively unscathed, with most buildings and homes still intact. Downtown Manila was a different story. A few weeks after the city was officially declared liberated, I saw the destruction firsthand. Papa Emilio and Joseling ventured into the city to check on relatives. Fueled by a sense of adventure and curiosity, I convinced them to let me come along. The Peñafiel relatives were among the fortunate families who survived the weeks of brutal fighting. But their neighborhood and surrounding area had been turned into a wasteland. Houses stood in pieces, their walls torn open like wounds. The ground was strewn with remnants of everyday life—pots, shoes, picture frames—now unrecognizable. Everywhere you looked, something was broken: a door dangling from its hinges, charred beams jutting skyward like dead fingers.

We considered ourselves lucky. By the grace of God, we still had a roof over our heads and beds to sleep in. Yet despite having shelter, poverty loomed. It could be weeks, even months, before anyone in the family found work. Most of the Peñafiels' prized possessions—jewelry, heirlooms, even furniture—had been traded away in the black market. Food and supplies trickled in from the provinces, but freedom didn't feed you. We were free—but still hungry.

Foraging, once a lifeline during the occupation, was no longer reliable. The land had been picked clean. We had to look elsewhere for sustenance. Word spread: the Americans had food.

After the fighting ceased, US Army camps sprang up across Manila and its outskirts. One of these olive-drab tent cities sprouted up near our neighborhood. Their presence was reassuring: friendly faces, calm voices, and a peaceful demeanor—a stark contrast to the scowls, shouts, and cruelty of the Japanese soldiers. This new occupying force brought safety, security—and something else: food.

I could smell the food from far away—different each day, unfamiliar but irresistible. The aromas were strange, nothing like the garlic and ginger of Mama Doray's kitchen in better days. But it was enticing, almost dizzying nevertheless.

It took a few days to gather the courage to get close to their camp. I lingered at the edges, watching, hoping no one would notice me. A quiet shame settled over me—had I been reduced to begging? I saw other kids doing the same, mostly younger ones, their mothers with them, faces filled with hunger and worry.

I eventually went up to the fence and stood, quiet and waiting, my hands clenched around the torn cloth of my skirt. One of the soldiers noticed me. He was older than the others, not quite Papa Emilio's age, with a kind smile and a funny way of talking I couldn't quite understand. He reached into his bag and pulled out a small piece of bread, tossing it to me with a wink. I caught it, my hands trembling. I held the bread like it was a treasure, a secret just for me.

I took a step back from the fence and turned around, suddenly feeling like I couldn't wait another second. I bit into the bread as I walked, savoring its taste and texture. The crisp crust and soft center filled my mouth, quieting the emptiness that had gnawed at me for weeks. I knew I should save it, bring it home, divide it among the others. But guilt was no match for hunger. During the war, I could rely on food at Millie's house to supplement the meager rations at home. But now that was gone. I was so hungry, hungrier than I'd ever been in my life. So, I kept eating, telling myself that maybe next time I'd bring something back for them.

The next day, I went again, my empty stomach leading me back to the fence. This time, I saw a different soldier, younger, with freckles and a hearty laugh. He handed me an open can with diced fruit in it. I accepted it timidly, feeling a thrill rise up inside me. I scooped the fruit with my fingers, each bite a burst of sweetness I hadn't tasted in years—it was intoxicating. As the juice dripped down my chin, I felt a wave of shame, knowing I should take it back to my family. But the hunger took over, and before I knew it, the canned fruit was gone.

I went back every few days, each time a little braver, each time telling myself I'd bring something back. The soldiers started to recognize me. Some were friendly, and others just walked past me, but they all seemed to understand why I was there. They'd give me bits of bread, sometimes a slice of meat, or even a piece of candy. I'd eat it all as soon as I could, too hungry to wait until I got home. I was alone, I told myself. My family didn't need to know.

After a couple of weeks, this developed into a routine for me and the other kids. By then, it seemed like many of the soldiers had grown weary of locals begging outside their camp. A few of them would still hand out whatever they had to spare, but most of them started to ignore us. I began to wonder if I needed a new approach.

One afternoon, I noticed an opening in the fence on the edge of the camp. With the ports open, supply runs were steady. Surely they had more food to spare. But the only way to find out would be to venture into the camp. It was risky, yes—but what was the worst that could happen? I was just a girl, hungry and curious. With the Japanese, a stunt like this would be unthinkable. But with the friendly Americans, I'd likely get off with a mild warning and be sent on my way. They might even get a good laugh out of it.

That afternoon, I nonchalantly sauntered over to the fence opening, hoping not to draw attention to myself. At this time of day, most of the soldiers were in the mess tent, so there weren't a lot of people around. I crouched low and slipped through the opening. Just like that, I was inside. A few feet away there was a row of tents. I headed toward the nearest one. The flaps were open and it appeared to be unattended—an invitation. My stomach growled as I imagined what might be inside—bread, fruit, maybe even one of those tins of meat that I'd only tasted once before. I looked around, then crept inside.

There was a small box in the corner. With my hands slightly trembling, I opened it and found a few cans. I couldn't read all of the labels but I knew they contained food. My heart raced. There was enough to share—maybe two cans, one for the family, one just for me.

Before I could decide, I heard footsteps behind me. I spun around, clutching the cans tightly to my chest, and came face-to-face with a soldier. He looked different from the others—his skin tone a bit darker. A mestizo, but not from our islands.

"What are you doing here?" he asked quietly.

I understood his English, but I didn't answer. I felt frozen, like my feet were glued to the ground. Maybe if I played dumb, like I didn't understand English, he would just let me go.

"Do you understand me? What are you doing here?" he asked again.

I remained motionless, fear and doubt starting to creep in. Sure, the Americans were friendlier than the Japanese, but maybe they'd be angry that I broke into their compound. Angry enough to turn me over to the local police, who wouldn't find my stunt amusing.

The soldier asked again, this time in Spanish.

"¿Habla español?"

I nodded my head sheepishly.

He sighed, took a step forward, and gently removed the cans from my hands. He placed them back in the box, his expression stern, yet sympathetic.

"You can't come back here, niña," he continued in Spanish, his voice almost a whisper. "It's not safe for you." He looked around, his eyes hardening, as if he saw things that weren't there.

I looked up at him, confused. "*¿Por qué?*"

He hesitated, glancing at me with a look I couldn't understand. "Some men here, they aren't all kind," he said finally, his voice low and deliberate. "Not everyone would treat you as a child who needs help. Some of them might…" he paused, the momentary silence carrying weight. "Some might try to take advantage."

Then, he reached into his own bag and handed me a tan, rectangular box, slightly larger than a shoe box. I didn't know for sure its contents, but the word printed in bold black letters on the box was unmistakable—dinner.

His face softened, and he seemed almost sad as he spoke. "Please, promise me you won't come back."

I didn't understand what he was talking about. These were American soldiers, the men who saved us from the Japanese. I wasn't supposed to be afraid of them. But something in his voice carried a tone of seriousness, an unspoken danger to be reckoned with. I nodded, holding the box tightly. He nodded back, and I could see he was relieved. Without another word, I turned and ran, slipping through the fence without detection.

Back at home, I handed the box to Mama Doray, her eyes lighting up as she took it, not asking where it came from. Among its contents was a can of stew and a bullion packet. Mama supplemented it with some camote leaves and potatoes she got from a neighbor. Dinner that night was a little heartier, thanks to the gift from the soldier.

As I lay in bed that night, my mind filled with questions about the soldier's cautionary words. For the first time, I felt something heavier than hunger, a weight I didn't understand but knew would stay with me. I thought of the concerned look on his face and his strange warning, a warning I didn't fully grasp but felt all the same.

25 An Unexpected Visitor

A couple of months had passed since liberation was declared in Manila, and life was beginning to return to some semblance of normalcy. Carlota and Tito had found secretarial jobs at a nearby US Army camp, which meant the family finally had an income again. Joseling helped relatives in the city clean up and rebuild what was left of their homes. Papa Emilio was still looking for work; unfortunately, the company he had worked for before the war had shut down. Still, we were confident he would find something eventually. Mama Doray continued her duties as homemaker and helped look after Carlota's younger children. Schools were slowly reopening, but I hadn't been enrolled yet, so I still had the freedom to roam around with the neighborhood kids. With the Japanese gone from our midst, we could reclaim our adventurous spirit—children without fear. I took full advantage of this freedom, knowing it was only a matter of time before Mama Doray put me on lockdown again.

One afternoon, while walking home after an expedition with my friends, we spotted something that made us stop in our tracks—a US Army jeep parked in front of the Peñafiel house, a soldier standing beside it.

"What do you think that's about?" Paco asked.

"I don't know," I said, shrugging.

I didn't really know what the US Army was doing at our house, but I had a theory. Maybe someone had reported me for sneaking into the camp weeks earlier. Maybe they were here for me.

My mind raced through worst-case scenarios. The moment I stepped inside, they'd grab me, throw me into the jeep, and haul me off for interrogation. Even if I hadn't actually stolen anything, I could still be punished—maybe jail, maybe hard labor. But I still had a chance to escape. I hadn't reached the front of the house yet. If I turned and ran, maybe I could get away.

"Let's go see what's going on," said Caloy.

"Nah, let's go to the creek instead," I suggested, trying to sound casual. "Maybe we'll find some frogs."

"We can do that anytime," Paco shot back. "Besides, they might have some candy."

My plan to steer them away failed. Before I could decide whether to bolt, I heard Papa Emilio's voice.

"Ging!" he called from the porch. "There's someone here to see you!"

Papa could clearly see I had returned from hanging out with my friends. Any hopes of escaping were quickly dashed. With my head hung low, I slowly walked toward the house.

"Wow! The US Army is here to see you!" exclaimed Paco. "What for?"

"Maybe she's getting a medal for secretly helping the guerillas!" joked Caloy.

In their excitement, neither of them noticed my lack of enthusiasm.

When we reached the porch, Papa Emilio sent the boys away.

"Ging has a visitor. Go home now. She can come out later."

Disappointed, Paco and Caloy hung back. But instead of going home, they wandered over to the soldier by the jeep, hoping for candy. I glanced at them briefly, then turned back to the house, my stomach twisting in nervous anticipation.

Inside, I saw a soldier seated on the sofa, Mama Doray across from him. He smiled—warm, easy—but I couldn't shake the suspicion. My heart thumped, a mixture of fear and curiosity. Was this some kind of trick?

I studied the soldier carefully. There seemed something vaguely familiar about him. He didn't look American. Handsome, tanned, with a pencil-thin mustache—like a mestizo version of Douglas Fairbanks Jr.

Papa Emilio stood beside me, hand on my shoulder. "Ging, this is your brother Ricardo."

I looked from Papa to the soldier seated in the living room, surprised. I'd never heard of this brother before. Maybe it really *was* a trick, designed to make me go along with them.

Ricardo stood and hugged me. I froze, unsure what to do.

"I'm so happy to finally meet you!" he said, his voice tinged with excitement. "Your Mama Caring will be happy to know you're doing well."

He noticed the confusion on my face and chuckled softly. "You're probably wondering about me and how we're related. Why don't we have a seat, and I'll explain everything?"

Although I remained skeptical, I was beginning to believe he hadn't come to arrest me after all. Ricardo and I sat on the sofa, Papa Emilio on a chair next to Mama Doray.

Ricardo began his story. His mother had been a domestic worker for Lola Julia, my Papa Peping's mother. She caught my father's eye, and even though he was already married, he pursued her. She became pregnant, and to avoid scandal, Lola Julia sent her to the province. After Ricardo was born, his mother struggled to raise him, so Lola Julia took him in. Later, Mama Caring learned about him but held no hard feelings—she treated him as her own son.

During the war, Ricardo joined the Philippine Scouts, a Filipino unit in the US Army. As the conflict continued, he stayed in touch with Mama Caring as best he could. After the hostilities ended, she asked him to find me, to make sure I was safe.

Ricardo continued with news about my family in Cebu.

"You'll be happy to know that everyone back in Cebu is

fine—they're all okay."

He went on to explain that, like much of the Philippines, Cebu endured hardship during the occupation. They too faced hunger and harassment from the Imperial Army. Eventually, they moved into one of the mountain provinces, where the Japanese forces were less present and food was easier to find.

I was relieved to hear the good news about my family. During the war, I had never stopped thinking about them—wondering if they were safe, if I'd ever see them again. I had no way of knowing.

And now, here was my brother Ricardo—someone I'd never known existed, suddenly becoming my lifeline to the family I'd missed so much.

It was overwhelming—discovering a brother I never knew, discovering that my family in Cebu had survived the war. I had so many questions, I didn't even know where to begin. In the absence of anything to ask, I just listened as Ricardo continued to speak.

He talked about Mama Caring and my brothers and sisters, mentioning them one by one. As he did, I tried to picture their faces, how different they might look now, how much older they must be. I wondered if they ever thought about me too, and how much I had changed since we last saw each other.

Ricardo paused, his cheerful tone faltering. I sensed that the next words would not be easy to hear.

"There's something else I need to tell you, Ging," he said gently. "It's about your Tio Meliton—the one married to your Tia Maria."

Tia Maria was one of Mama Caring's sisters. Her husband, my Tio Meliton Caballes, was a Corporal in the US Army—a Philippine Scout, like Ricardo. He was stationed at Fort McKinley, on the outskirts of Manila. Being my closest relatives in the area, Tio Meliton and Tia Maria often visited me, at Mama Caring's request.

As Ricardo continued, my stomach tightened. Something in his voice made me uneasy.

"During the Battle of Corregidor, he was captured along with the other American and Filipino soldiers and held as prisoners at Camp

O'Donnell. Many didn't survive… and I'm afraid your Tio Meliton was among them."

The words hit me like a cold wave. My chest felt tight, my hands went numb. I wanted to cry, to scream, to run away—but then a memory flickered through my mind. Tio Meliton and Tia Maria visiting me, smiling and carrying small bags from the PX on base. The treats! Candy bars I had never tasted before, and corn flakes—something I had never eaten in my life. I laugh even now remembering how I didn't know you were supposed to eat it with milk, and just crunched through it dry, delighted anyway.

At the time, I didn't fully understand the circumstances of Tio Meliton's death. I was still young, and much of the war's ugliness felt blurred and distant, as if they belonged to someone else's story.

It wasn't until years later, when I was grown, that I learned what really happened at Bataan. How thousands of Filipino and American soldiers, weak from hunger and disease, were forced to march for days under the scorching sun. Those who fell behind were beaten, or worse. Out of roughly 75,000 who began that march, barely more than half made it to the prison camps alive. Of those who made it to the camps, upwards of 20,000 eventually died in captivity due to disease, starvation, and the continued brutality of the Japanese.

I remember reading about it long after the war and realizing: my Tio Meliton was one of them. One of the men whose courage was never recorded in the history books, whose names faded even as their families grieved quietly at home.

When I think of him now, I still see the gentle man who brought me candy bars from the PX, the one who laughed when I crunched through corn flakes dry because I didn't know any better. I want to remember him that way—not as a prisoner of war, but as the uncle who delivered joy into my childhood.

Ricardo's hand rested lightly on mine, steady and comforting. "I'm so sorry, Ging. It must be difficult to imagine. I didn't know your Tio Meliton personally, but those who spoke of him said he was a good man and a brave soldier. We'll always remember him in our hearts."

Tears blurred my vision as I fought to keep from sobbing out loud. I tried to recall the last time I saw him, to bring back the warmth of his smile. I thought of my Tia Maria, the pain she must have carried, the struggle to raise their children without him. Ricardo reassured me that Tia Maria and her children had survived the war and made it back to Cebu, closer to family. I was grateful to hear that, even as I knew she would never fully recover from her loss.

We all sat in silence for a moment, Ricardo's hand still resting on mine. The room felt heavy with unspoken things—sorrow, gratitude, the fragile quiet that follows bad news. Outside, the wind stirred through the trees, carrying faint laughter from the neighborhood kids—a reminder that life, somehow, was already moving on.

Ricardo cleared his throat softly, gently interrupting the stillness in the room. He drew in a breath and managed a slight smile. "Before I forget," he said, "I brought some gifts."

He reached into his pack and began to pull out some items. "These aren't much," he said, "but I thought you might like them."

He handed me a chocolate bar—its smooth wrapper bearing the unmistakable name *Hershey's*. "For you, Ging. Something sweet to remember me by," he said with a wink. I held it close to my chest, and for a moment I felt like a little child again, back in the days before the war.

For Mama Doray, he set down a small sack with a few dry and canned goods—a much-needed boost to our pantry. She smiled and offered a 'Salamat' in gratitude.

And for Papa Emilio, a pack of Lucky Strikes. He chuckled approvingly, tucking it into his shirt pocket. "Thank you, Ricardo," he said, patting him gently on the shoulder.

"It's getting late, and I really must be getting back to camp now," Ricardo announced.

We all got up and started walking him to the door. Ricardo turned to me and opened his arms. I rushed forward, and he held me close—a strong, steady embrace that said everything words could not.

"I'll see you again, Ging," he whispered. "Soon, I promise."

I nodded, though I knew how uncertain "soon" could be in times like these. Still, I held on to his promise as I watched him walk out the door toward the jeep and his fellow soldier.

The sun dipped behind the trees, the sky turning amber—soft and hazy. The air smelled faintly of smoke and moist earth from the earlier rain. I stood by the doorway, watching as Ricardo got in the jeep. He smiled and waved. As I waved back, the jeep rumbled to life, coughing out smoke from its exhaust.

I watched as it rolled down the road, shrinking until it disappeared into the haze.

When he finally vanished from view, I stood there a little longer, holding the chocolate bar against my chest, as if by doing so I could hold on to him too.

Long after he was gone, I stayed by the doorway, watching the road fade into dusk. The war had taken so much, yet in that moment, I realized it hadn't taken everything. I still had family—scattered, changed, but alive—and the fragile thread of hope that one day we'd all find our way back to each other.

26 Cebu Bound

Ricardo's visit brought a mix of feelings. I was elated to learn I had another brother—a soldier—someone who helped liberate us from the Japanese. I was also overjoyed to learn that my real parents, and my siblings, had survived the war and were safe back in Cebu. All these new emotions made me reflect on my life here in Manila.

The Peñafiels had practically raised me since I was a baby. Mama Doray and Papa Emilio treated me like one of their own. I thought of them as my parents and their children as my brothers and sisters. Carlota's children even called me Tita Ging—a title I had been proud to carry since I was eight years old.

Yet I always knew this was not a permanent arrangement. The Peñafiels weren't my real family. Whenever Mama Caring visited me before the war, she reminded me of that—and that one day she would come to bring me home for good. But those plans were put on hold.

For four years, Mama Caring lived in a limbo of silence, not knowing if I was alive or dead. It had been years since we'd last seen each other, but she clung to the hope that I was safe in Manila with the Peñafiels. After hearing about the carnage from the Battle of Manila, she told me later, she held on to a fragile hope but feared the worst.

During the war, she understood that communication was nearly impossible. But as peace returned and letters began to find their way to long-separated families, she grew more anxious with each passing month. Why hadn't the Peñafiels reached out? Surely, they could have sent word to let her know I was safe.

Finally, after what must have been an agonizing wait, Mama Caring learned, through Ricardo, that I had survived war. A week later, she sent the Peñafiels a letter, telling them she would soon be coming to Manila to bring me back to Cebu.

Mama Doray and Papa Emilio were devastated by the news. Mama Doray took it especially hard. I could see it in her face and hear it in her tone during conversations I overheard, unbeknownst to them.

"How can Caring do this?" she protested to Papa Emilio. "We raised her. We're the only family she knows."

"I know, Doray, but what can we do?" replied Papa Emilio. "Caring is her real mother. Besides, we knew this day would come."

"In our hearts, Ging will always be our daughter," he added softly, as consolation.

I was torn—caught in the middle of an emotional tug of war. On one hand, I longed to be reunited with my family in Cebu. But on the other hand, I felt just as much a part of the Peñafiel family. I knew them better than my real family. We had a bond as strong, if not stronger, than any blood tie—one strengthened by the harshness of war.

Yet in spite of that closeness, I couldn't deny the quiet pull inside me—the feeling that maybe it was time to be with my Mama Caring and the rest of my family.

The weeks leading up to my departure were emotionally tough. A heaviness settled over the Peñafiel home. Everyone knew I was leaving, but no one talked about it. Life went on as if everything was fine—but it wasn't.

Mama Doray was quieter than usual. I sensed that she was distancing herself from me, as if trying to get used to my absence before I was even gone. The silence was painful. I wanted her to be happy for me—that I would finally be reunited with my family.

Instead, it felt as though she were punishing me for abandoning them.

When Mama Caring finally arrived at their doorstep, they greeted her with restrained politeness and superficial hugs. The tension was palpable. They treated her almost as an intruder rather than the mother who had come to reclaim her daughter.

As soon as Mama Caring entered the house, her expression softened. At first, she wore a stoic, tired look, but when she saw me, her eyes lit up. We rushed toward each other and embraced tightly. Tears flowed freely, releasing years of fear and separation. The embrace felt warm but foreign, as if both of us were trying to find the pieces that had been misplaced over the years. The war had changed us both, but it couldn't erase the bond between mother and daughter.

She took a step back and held my face in her hands.

"My little girl!" she exclaimed. "You've grown so much!"

"And still as beautiful as ever," she added, wiping my tears.

I caught a glimpse of Mama Doray and Papa Emilio from the corner of my eye. Papa managed a slight smile. He was saddened by my impending departure, but I knew he was touched by the sight of my reunion with my birth mother. Mama Doray's expression remained stern; she turned away when our eyes met.

The reunion at the Peñafiel home didn't last long. Mama Caring had written that she didn't plan to stay—only long enough to collect me and my few remaining possessions. There was no need for a going-away party, not that Mama Doray was in any mood to host one. Mama Caring also made it clear that we wouldn't need accommodations, since we would be staying with relatives until our departure.

When it was time to go, the entire Peñafiel family gathered in the living room. I hugged each of them as we said our goodbyes.

When it was Papa Emilio's turn, I wrapped my arms around him and held on tightly. The tears began to flow again. He stroked my hair and whispered, "There, there, mija. Don't be sad. I'll write you—so you make sure to write me back, okay?"

I nodded and looked up at him. Papa Emilio was never one to show emotion, but for a moment I caught something in his eyes—a quiet sorrow he could not hide.

Then I went to Mama Doray and gave her a hug. She hugged me back, but it felt almost perfunctory.

"I'll miss you, Mama," I said, hoping for some sign of warmth.

"You be a good girl, okay?" she replied. "And make sure to pray the Rosary."

"It's time to go now, Ging," Mama Caring said softly. "There's a taxi waiting."

Everyone stood by the door as Joseling helped us load our things. Mama Caring and I lingered by the taxi while I took one last look at my adoptive family and waved goodbye. As we drove away, I looked back at them through the rear window. Their faces were heavy with sadness—all except for Mama Doray, whose expression remained unreadable.

The next day, we boarded a ferry bound for Cebu—a journey toward reunion, but also farewell. I felt so many mixed emotions that I could barely sleep the entire trip. For as long as I could remember, Manila had been my home, even though it was far from where I was born. The Peñafiels had taken me in as a child and raised me as their own. Their kindness had been a gift: they fed and clothed me, taught me right from wrong, and loved me as parents should. I loved them in return.

I was leaving them to be with my family—but I wasn't leaving them behind. They would always be with me, carried in a special place in my heart.

27 Homecoming

I had imagined this day for years—the moment I would finally come home. It was early 1946, and Cebu felt like a different world. I was only eight when I left for Manila, so my memories of what it was like were vague—just flashes of narrow streets, the clang of church bells, and the scent of dried fish curling through the market stalls. Manila, at least before the war, was more modern and cosmopolitan: wide boulevards, electric lights, and the clank and squeal of streetcars echoing down the tracks.

Though not quite a metropolis, Cebu City was a vital cultural and commercial hub in the central Visayas. Compared to Manila, it had always felt quieter, more intimate—a city that moved to its own rhythm. Before the war, it was a place of merchants and fishermen, of Chinese shopkeepers and Spanish stone churches, where the sea was never far and the language of home—*Cebuano*—wrapped around me like a lullaby.

As I stepped off the ferry, the salt air hit me, sharp and familiar. I saw a city changed by occupation and survival, but still pulsing with the same stubborn warmth. It was hard to tell if I was returning after a long absence or arriving for the first time.

My older brother Julio was waiting for me and Mama at the port. He was no longer the boy I used to hunt frogs with and play alongside in the river near our house. Julio had grown into a handsome young man—strong, with broad shoulders and a hint of facial hair. He rushed up to us, hugging Mama Caring first, then me.

"Look at you, Ging! All grown up!"

I smiled. Even though he was my brother, I felt a little shy and didn't know what to say.

After he helped us load our bags into a waiting kalesa, we headed toward our house on Sikatuna Street. During the ride, he asked about our trip, then filled me in on the family events I had missed while I was away. He talked about brothers and sisters—some I barely remembered, as if they had existed only in a dream. Others were too young, or not even born yet, when I left.

Julio also asked about life in Manila with the Peñafiels. He was curious about "the big city" and how the Peñafiels treated me. He asked about the war too—was it just as bad in Manila as it was in Cebu?

Although I wasn't in a very talkative mood, I answered his questions politely, if briefly. Julio was obviously excited to see me, and I was happy to see him too—just quieter about it. Maybe it was exhaustion, both physical and emotional, from the journey. Or maybe I was simply overwhelmed by how much everything had changed.

The kalesa rattled through the narrow streets, past familiar corners that seemed both new and remembered. As we turned onto Sikatuna, my pulse quickened. Then, there it was—the house I had pictured so many times in my mind.

The house was bustling, nothing like the Peñafiel household I'd known. My family's home in Cebu was smaller, but it pulsed with life. Siblings bickered over space at the table, elbows jostling. There was laughter, and sometimes, too, a silence that came from our strange mixture of closeness and distance. In Manila, everything had been quiet, orderly, and structured, but here, life was vibrant and chaotic—like a dance with too many partners.

At first, as I watched my siblings interact, I wasn't quite sure where I fit in. Nene and Benjie would tease each other, arguing about who could catch more fish or climb trees higher. My sisters—Nena,

Helen, Penang, and Julia—greeted me with openness and warmth. They had all grown up to be beautiful young women. To make me feel at home, they teased me too, joking about their newly arrived sister, the "big city mestiza from Manila." I felt an immediate kinship with them.

I also got to meet my two younger sisters for the first time, Susan (whom we called Sunny) and Josefina (Pina). Sunny was around seven, and Pina two when I returned to Cebu. They both greeted me with hugs, but for the first couple of days, they shied away, watching from a distance. Their eyes were full of curiosity—and something else I couldn't place. I often caught them looking at me when they thought I wasn't paying attention. It didn't take long, however, for them to warm up—and soon they were laughing and playing with me, just like my other siblings.

Despite the clamor and the initial unfamiliarity, something settled in my chest. There was a warmth, a fullness I hadn't realized was missing in Manila. Slowly, I found my rhythm, doing chores, caring for my younger siblings, and attending school. I especially enjoyed bonding with Mama Caring and my sisters in the kitchen—getting reacquainted with each other and learning to cook dishes I hadn't tasted in years.

The days turned into weeks, and my life in Cebu grew roots. Each of us carried scars from the war, but we healed together. We would sit outside in the evenings, watching the stars, each with our own stories but somehow connected under the same sky. The Peñafiels had given me a home, food, and kindness, but it was here—amid the joyful noise and sibling squabbles—that I felt a deeper warmth, a feeling I could only call family.

28 Inez

As I settled into my new life back in Cebu, I began to connect with members of my extended family—siblings my father had with another woman, Inez. Peping and Inez had five children together: Carlos, Julia, Salvador, Susan (Sunny), and Josefina (Pina). They were close in age to Mama Caring's children; in fact, Julia and I were only a few weeks apart.

Despite the unconventional nature of our family dynamic, the interactions among all of us siblings felt natural, almost effortless. Mama Caring, ever gracious, made it a point to emphasize that we were never to refer to one another as "half-brothers" or "half-sisters." She firmly believed that we were all children of Jose Ramon Moro and equally deserving of love and belonging. Her resolve created a sense of unity that transcended the circumstances of our shared history.

I hadn't yet met Inez, and the thought of her lingered in my mind like an unanswered question. There was an undeniable air of mystery about the woman who had been such a pivotal figure in my father's life. When Mama Caring told me that Inez would be joining us for dinner, my heart fluttered with a mixture of curiosity and nervous anticipation.

Mama Caring had always spoken kindly of Inez, never with a trace of bitterness or resentment. Her warmth remained steadfast, even toward the woman whose presence could have easily unraveled our family. "Inez is family, too," she said simply, as if to reassure me.

Yet, I couldn't help but feel a swirl of emotions—intrigue mingled with unease. This was the woman who had shared my father's love, a man who had scattered pieces of himself across many places, leaving a mark on the hearts of both Mama Caring and Inez. Meeting her felt inevitable, but I wondered what it would reveal about the man who had bound us all together.

Meeting Inez felt like discovering a hidden chapter in a beloved book I thought I knew by heart. That evening, as the sun melted into the horizon, Inez arrived at our house. She stepped through the door with a quiet charm that immediately drew your attention. I understood at once why my father had been attracted to her. She radiated a timeless beauty, as if she had stepped out of an old Hollywood film. Her delicate, Eurasian features were striking: a porcelain-like complexion, glossy black hair that cascaded in soft waves, and dark almond-shaped eyes that accentuated her exotic allure.

I hesitated as I approached her, unsure of how to bridge the gap between us. But Inez met me halfway with a soft smile that dissolved some of my apprehension. Her gaze held a tenderness that felt almost familiar, like she had known me all my life. Reaching out, she gently placed a hand on my cheek, her touch warm and light.

"Ging—you are even more beautiful than I imagined!" she said, her voice carrying a gentle lilt. Then she pulled me into an embrace, her arms wrapping around me with a surprising firmness that felt both comforting and intimate. In that hug, I sensed the weight of a lifetime's worth of unspoken stories and unshared moments—a connection we were only just beginning to explore.

Over dinner, we shared food and laughter, though it felt surreal to sit at the table with both my mother and Inez. I watched them exchange glances—sometimes silent, sometimes accompanied by shared laughter—as if they were co-conspirators in the intricate love story they had both endured. Yet, the atmosphere was anything but tense. Inez listened intently as my mother told stories about our family, nodding along as though she had lived those moments herself. In a sense, she had—though her part in the narrative had remained hidden from me until now.

After the meal, we washed and put away the dishes together, an unspoken collaboration that felt strangely harmonious. Later, my mother and Inez settled on the front porch, their voices mingling with the sounds of the warm Cebu evening. They chatted and laughed, more like old friends than women whose lives had been entangled by my father's choices. It was a scene I knew I would carry with me forever: two women bound by shared pain, yet capable of finding something beautiful in their connection.

That night, after Inez had gone home, I asked my mother how she had come into our lives. Mama Caring didn't hesitate; it was clear this was a story she had told many times before, each retelling smoothing its jagged edges.

Years before the war, my father had met Inez on a ferry during one of his business trips. She had been fleeing a life of misery—a marriage to an abusive husband and a mother-in-law who treated her like an outsider in her own home. Inez was desperate to return to Guam, her homeland, but lacked the means to get there. When she crossed paths with my father, he must have sensed her despair. He was, after all, a man who never turned away from a beautiful woman in need.

My father promised her safety and pledged to help her return to Guam. Peping was charming, and he made Inez feel seen, valued. She believed him when he said he could help her. Of course, he didn't tell her he was already married.

He assured Inez it would take some time to arrange her return to Guam, convincing her to stay in Cebu in the meantime. He even set her up with a place of her own. As a traveling salesman, it was easy for Peping to visit her often, and their relationship deepened. Then came the children, one after another.

For years, Inez clung to the hope that my father would fulfill his promise to take her back to Guam. But as time passed, it became clear he had other obligations—obligations he had kept hidden from her. With a growing family in Cebu, her dream of returning to Guam slowly faded, replaced by the reality of the life she had built here.

"When did you find out, Mama?" I asked her.

She told me she had suspected for some time that Peping was involved with another woman, but she never confronted him. She preferred to pretend that nothing was amiss in their marriage, holding onto a fragile semblance of normalcy.

Then one day, a group of neighborhood women approached her, their words sharp and unrelenting.

"Peping has taken up with another woman right under your nose! And you do nothing? He's even fathered children with her! He doesn't even bother to hide it—everyone in the neighborhood knows! For the sake of your dignity, Caring, do something about it!"

Their accusations were persistent, forcing her to face a truth she had been avoiding. The revelation cut deep, sparking anger and humiliation she could no longer suppress. The women pressed on, fanning the flames of her anguish.

"Her name is Inez, and we know where she and her children live. Let's go there and teach her a lesson. No one would blame you—not a judge, not a jury."

The name struck like a thunderbolt: Inez, the woman who had shared my father's love and borne his children. Normally docile and passive, Mama Caring was now consumed by a storm of anger. It was a rage born of betrayal, anguish, and a desperate desire for retribution.

With the neighbor women as her allies, my mother began plotting. They convinced themselves that revenge was the only justice for the pain Inez's presence had caused. Their hearts burned with bitterness as they conspired to expose her, to inflict upon her the suffering they believed she deserved. Their resolve seemed unshakable.

Later that night, the women presented my mother with a bolo knife—the tool they believed would bring closure. Mama Caring, still engulfed in anger, took the knife in her trembling hands. Together, they made their way to Inez's home, ready to carry out their plan.

But fate has a way of intervening. As they stood outside Inez's house, the flicker of light from a window caught my mother's attention. Peering inside, she saw Inez sitting in a chair, cradling a nursing infant in her arms. The scene was serene—mother and child bathed in the soft glow of lamplight, oblivious to the storm brewing just outside.

In that moment, something shifted in my mother's heart. She saw the child's face, so innocent and peaceful, so much like her own baby daughter Ging. The sheer vulnerability of the infant tugged at her conscience, dissolving the hardened resolve etched by betrayal. The anger that had consumed her began to ebb, replaced by a profound sense of compassion.

As she stood there, the knife still in her hand, she made a choice—a choice to release her rage and the bitter need for revenge. She saw Inez not as an enemy, but as another victim caught in Peping's web of deception. The pain that united them outweighed the divides between them.

With a heavy heart and newfound clarity, my mother lowered the knife. She and the other women retreated into the night, abandoning their plans for revenge. They realized that vengeance would only perpetuate the cycle of suffering, trapping them all in darkness.

Ashamed of what they had almost done, my mother and the others never spoke of that night again. Over time, my father's "secret" family became known, and, out of necessity—especially during the war—the two families merged in an unconventional coexistence.

Mama Caring came to understand that Inez, like her, had been swept into Peping's charm and restlessness. Inez was not a rival or an enemy; she was a fellow traveler on a path shaped by his betrayals. My mother chose forgiveness over hatred, drawing strength from shared pain and loss. Though the scars of betrayal never fully faded, they served as a testament to the resilience it took to turn away from vengeance and toward compassion.

After learning about her backstory, I found myself increasingly drawn to Inez. She carried a quiet resilience, a grace that came from enduring hardship without letting it harden her spirit. There was a warmth in her gestures, a kindness that lingered despite the challenges she had faced.

Sometimes, on my way home from school, Inez would call out to me and ask me to stop by.

"Are you hungry? Let me fix you something to eat," she would say with a gentle smile.

During these visits, I would sit and listen as she shared stories of Guam, the island where she had grown up, and the family she had left behind. In her words, I glimpsed her strength—an unwavering will to adapt and persevere. But beneath her strength lay a poignant vulnerability, a quiet sadness. She spoke of Guam with a longing that deepened with each passing year, her dreams of returning growing fainter like a ship disappearing into the horizon.

And there was something else. Despite my mother's open-hearted acceptance, I could sense that Inez often felt like she would always be an outsider. It was an ache she never voiced but that lingered in her gaze and softened her smile—a reminder of how deeply her life had been shaped by choices beyond her control.

As I got to know Inez, I felt an unexpected kinship with her. It became clear why Mama Caring had chosen not to hold a grudge against her. My mother and Inez became pillars in my life— two women bound not only by the same man but by a shared resilience that transcended their circumstances.

Each of them imparted something precious to me: from my mother, I learned the power of forgiveness; from Inez, the strength of perseverance with grace. Together, they shaped my understanding of love, endurance, and the complexities of family.

Between them, I discovered not only the depth of my roots but also a profound sense of belonging. They created a space large enough to hold us all, no matter how tangled and complicated our story might have been.

29 Discomforts Of Home

Some events in life have a honeymoon phase—a period of intense happiness, excitement, and a tendency to overlook flaws. Eventually, reality sets in, and you see things as they really are. It wasn't long after my return to Cebu that the initial euphoria began to wear off, and the excitement of being back home with my family started to fade.

As much as I loved my brothers and sisters, the cramped living quarters were beginning to take their toll. With so many people in the house, there was no room for beds, so we had to sleep on the floor. We lay almost shoulder-to-shoulder on *banig* (woven palm mats), packed like sardines. At first it seemed fun and cozy, sharing girl talk with my sisters before drifting off to sleep. But after several nights of elbows in the face and being awakened by nearby snoring, the charm quickly faded.

At first, I loved the noise—the chatter of my siblings, the creak of floorboards, the laughter spilling from one room to another. It made the house feel alive in a way the Peñafiel home never did. But after a few weeks, that same clamor started to grate on me. There was never a moment of quiet. Someone was always talking, yelling, or laughing, and even the smallest movement seemed amplified in the close quarters. I found myself longing for a corner to think, to read, or just to breathe. The lively household I once yearned for now felt confining, and I realized that constant closeness came with its own kind of exhaustion.

Our home in Cebu was not only crowded but also lacked the comforts I had taken for granted in Manila. We had no indoor bathroom, which meant showering outside and, even worse, having to use the stinky outhouse out back. I hated it.

One particularly humid morning, after a restless night of elbows to the face, I went to the outside shower to freshen up before school. I needed to do "number two" badly but dreaded enduring the stench of the outhouse. As the cool water poured over me, I weighed my options. In my desperation to avoid it, I made a terrible decision. I took a quick peek to make sure no one was around, then squatted down in the shower and let nature take its course.

When I stood up, the water rushed away, carrying my indiscretion—or so I thought. I had misjudged the slope of the narrow drainage trench. The water wasn't strong enough, and my poop got stuck halfway down. I was horrified. When—*not if*—someone found it, there would be hell to pay. I finished rinsing off, toweled dry in record time, and hurried back inside.

Moments later, I heard Julio's voice booming outside.

"*Bastos!*" he bellowed, his voice full of disgust.

I peeked out the window and saw him glaring down at the trench where my "package" was stuck.

"Who the hell took a crap in the shower?" he shouted.

I ducked back into the room, heart pounding.

"If I find out who did this, I'll make you pick it up with your hands!" he yelled before storming off.

Penang, who was in the room with me, burst into giggles. She knew. Embarrassed, I finished getting dressed, and we walked to school without a word. She never told anyone. Years later, it became a family joke—something we'd laugh about at get-togethers, though I still felt my cheeks burn every time it came up.

The neighborhood surrounding our home added another layer of discomfort. It was known for its reputation—a place where women walked the streets under cover of night, offering companionship to inebriated men wandering in search of pleasure. I often watched from the safety of the bedroom window, heart pounding as shadows flitted past the front of our house. The drunken laughter and shouted propositions seeped in like the humid air. Walking home after visiting friends was always unsettling. Even though none of us girls ever went out alone, safety in numbers didn't always feel safe. It was a danger I didn't fully understand but felt keenly aware of all the same.

One day, Joseling and Manoling (Tito's husband) came to visit while their ship was docked in Cebu. They were merchant seamen whose voyages took them around the world. Papa Emilio—whom I was writing to regularly since leaving Manila—had told me they would be stopping by. I was thrilled to see someone from the Peñafiel family. Even though I was receiving letters often, it would be comforting to see one of them in person.

I waited out front as they walked up the street. I could read the concern on their faces as they took in the rowdy neighborhood, but their expressions softened into warm smiles the moment they saw me. They greeted me with hugs, and I welcomed them inside for refreshments. As we caught up, I noticed their eyes quietly taking in the surroundings—the crowded living room, the constant chatter, the noise that had once felt joyful but now grated at times. They exchanged worried glances but said nothing.

When Mama Caring invited them to stay for dinner, they politely declined, saying they were meeting shipmates before returning to port. I was quietly relieved. The thought of them sitting at our loud, crowded table made me anxious. We said our goodbyes, and they promised to visit again next time they docked in Cebu.

A few weeks later, a letter arrived from Papa Emilio. My heart raced as I unfolded the paper. His handwriting was as steady and familiar as ever. He wrote that Joseling and Manoling had told him about my living conditions, and he asked gently if I wanted to return to Manila.

The question hung heavy in the air. I pictured my life there: the neatness of Mama Doray's home, the safety of the bus ride to school, the absence of drunken laughter at night. But alongside that image was the warmth of my family here—the laughter, the teasing, the chaos that somehow felt like love.

After nights of turning it over in my mind, I wrote back with trembling hands. I told him yes—I wanted to return to Manila. As I sealed the envelope, a weight settled in my stomach. I knew I was choosing safety over the chaos I had just reentered, but my heart ached for what I was leaving behind. I closed my eyes and promised myself that no matter where I went, a part of me would always stay with my family in Cebu.

30 The Long Walk

When I returned to the Peñafiel home in San Juan, it almost felt as if I had never left. I was thrilled to be back in my room, enjoying the space and privacy I had missed in Cebu.

Papa Emilio and the rest of the family were ecstatic to have me back, their warm welcomes making it clear. Mama Doray, however, was more restrained. I'm sure she was happy I had returned, but she didn't make a show of it. I almost sensed her private satisfaction, a quiet "See, I knew you would come back."

She wasted no time getting me back into my old routine—chores, homework, and helping in the kitchen. I had hoped for a small break, but Mama Doray's stern nature wouldn't allow it.

Not long after, she had me accompany her to the market, just like before. That day, the heat and humidity were relentless. The sun blazed overhead, pressing down from all sides. My dress clung to my back, soaked with sweat, and even the smallest movement seemed to thicken the air around me. I wiped my forehead with the back of my hand, but it did little. The sticky heat wrapped around me like a second skin, unyielding and suffocating.

The path home felt endless, the dirt beneath our feet kicking up small puffs of dust as we walked, the road ahead shimmering with reflected heat. Mama Doray had me carry the basket, heavy with the week's groceries—vegetables, dried fish, and a few eggs carefully cradled in the folds of a cloth. She walked slightly ahead, her steps steady and graceful, unaffected by the sweltering air.

My feet ached, and the thought of the long road ahead made me sigh. That was when I spotted the kalesa, its wooden wheels creaking as it passed, the driver lazily flicking the reins. It moved slowly, almost at our pace, and in that moment, it felt like a gift from the heavens.

I looked at Mama Doray, hopeful. "Mama," I said, "can we ride the kalesa? Just this once?"

She didn't answer at first, just kept walking, her eyes straight ahead. I thought maybe she hadn't heard me, so I asked again, louder this time. "Mama, please? It's so hot."

Mama glanced at me, her face unreadable. "We don't have money for that, anak," she said softly but firmly.

Disappointment welled up in me—a frustration caused by the heat and Mama Doray's persistent need to stretch every peso. I opened my mouth to argue, but before I could, the kalesa driver slowed his horse and turned toward us.

He was a middle-aged man, his skin weathered from years in the sun, his shirt stained with sweat and dirt. "*Manang*, you two look tired," he said with a friendly grin. "Why don't you ride with me? I'm heading in the same direction anyway. No charge."

I looked at Mama, expecting agreement. The offer was kind and seemingly without strings. But Mama didn't smile. She stopped and adjusted the kerchief over her head. "No, thank you," she said, polite but firm. "We'll manage."

I stared at her, dumbfounded. The driver raised his eyebrows in surprise, but he didn't push. With a small nod, he flicked the reins and the cart moved on, the clop of hooves fading into the distance.

As we started walking again, I couldn't hold back my frustration. "Why didn't we take the ride, Mama?" I asked, my voice sharper than I intended. "He was just being nice. It was free."

Mama didn't look at me. She kept walking, eyes fixed ahead. After a pause, she spoke, quiet but firm. "Nothing's free, anak. Not from men."

I was confused by her words. "But he didn't want anything," I argued. "He was just offering to help."

Mama stopped and faced me, her expression serious, her tone stern. "You're young," she said softly. "You don't understand yet. Men don't give things away for nothing. They always want something in return. Always."

I nodded, though my mind buzzed with unanswered questions. To me, it seemed unfair. Yet Mama Doray had that look on her face—the one that told me not to question her, not now.

We walked the rest of the way in silence. The sun had begun to dip low, casting long shadows over the dirt path. The heat lingered, but the evening's coolness was slowly creeping in. My feet hurt and my back ached; I was too fatigued to ask again about the kalesa.

As we returned home, I struggled to understand Mama Doray's words. Was there some hidden message I'd missed? Or was this her way of punishing me for returning to Cebu? As a teenage girl, hot and tired from the walk home, all I saw was a lost opportunity for a free ride. It would be years before I fully understood Mama Doray's lesson that day.

31 Sweet Taste Of Rebellion

When I returned to San Juan, Mama Doray enrolled me at Our Lady of Loreto, the same Catholic school Jun and Mits—Carlota's son and daughter—attended. One of my responsibilities in the Peñafiel household was to look after them before and after class. They were well-behaved children, really. If anything, I was the one who needed supervision.

Our Lady of Loreto was typical of its time: nuns with ruler taps and murmured prayers, doing their best to keep us in line. But I was never one to be fully contained. There was always a scheme brewing, some mischief waiting to unfold—a constant source of frustration for Mama Doray.

The lunches we brought from home were modest: a pandesal roll with a thin smear of butter. Just enough to quiet our stomachs, never enough to satisfy. By the time classes ended, we were usually still hungry. One morning, I hatched a plan to fix that.

"How would you guys like a treat after school?" I whispered to Jun and Mits as we rode the bus.

Jun raised an eyebrow. "What do you mean?"

"We have money, right? Our bus fare. What if, instead of riding home, we use it to buy something better—like Pepsi and cookies?"

Mits, ever the cautious one, frowned. "But if we skip the bus... won't the walk home be too far, Tita?"

I waved off her concern. "Bah! It's not that far. You walk all over town with Lola Doray when you go to the market. Besides, you've got strong legs. That walk will be nothing."

Jun was already picturing the crunch of cookies and the fizz of cold soda. "Tita's right, Mits. It's not that long a walk—we can handle it."

"I guess the walk wouldn't be so bad," Mits said, her eyes lighting up. "And Pepsi with cookies sounds really good!"

I smiled, pleased at how easily they'd come around.

As the bus rattled toward school, I laid out the plan. Across the street from the stop was a sari-sari store, a red-white-and-blue Pepsi sign hanging proudly in the window. After school, we'd walk to the store and spend our fare on a bottle of soda and a bag of cookies to share. It was a simple plan—daring with a sweet payoff, and just mischievous enough to make the day memorable.

Minutes after the bell rang, we gathered by the heavy wooden school doors and crossed the street. Without hesitation, I stepped up to the counter, handed over our bus fare, and asked for a bottle of Pepsi and a small bag of cookies. Careful not to drop our precious cargo, I rejoined Jun and Mits at a nearby bench.

As their self-appointed leader, I took the first sip. That mouthful of fizzy goodness was so satisfying on that hot, sticky afternoon—the sweet taste of rebellion. I handed the bottle to Jun, who took his sip with a look of utter contentment. Then Mits followed, every bit as pleased by the bubbly, thirst-quenching drink. We continued this rotation, alternating between sips and munching on the crispy sugar cookies. For a brief moment, we were in our own little world, relishing the simple joy of breaking the rules.

When the bottle and bag were finally empty, we paused, each of us belching from the carbonation before bursting into laughter. Then we got up, tossed the empty containers into a nearby trash bin, and began our walk home.

At first, it seemed easy enough. The sun was still high in the sky, but a light breeze tempered the heat. Soon, though, the road seemed to stretch endlessly ahead, and the afternoon heat settled heavily on our shoulders. Only then did it hit me—home wasn't just a short stroll away. It was a long, sun-drenched stretch of road, and we were barely halfway there.

As the three of us trudged along, dust clung to our legs and passing cars belched exhaust in our faces. The sun was beating down on us, turning our once-fun adventure into a slow, exhausting journey.

"How much longer, Tita?" Mits kept asking, dragging her feet, her voice thin with exhaustion.

"Just a little bit more," I said, though even I didn't believe it. I was tired and irritated, but I also felt sorry for my young niece. After all, this was my doing.

I looked over at Jun. He was a good soldier, pressing forward, barely saying a word. At this point, I wanted to complain too, but kept it to myself. My shirt clung to my back, damp with sweat, and my feet ached with every step. The thrill of rebellion had begun to wear thin.

Back at home, Mama Doray was beginning to worry. She stood at the front of the house, eyes scanning the horizon for the familiar sight of the bus. When the first one passed without us, she thought nothing of it—maybe we'd missed it. But when the second came and went, still no sign of her kids, concern began to set in. By the third pass, she flagged down the driver, who shook his head and said we hadn't boarded. For Mama Doray, concern turned to dread.

"Where could they be?" she muttered, pacing the yard. Mama had always been a patient woman, but when it came to us, her patience thinned quickly when fear took over.

By the time we finally reached the end of our block, the sun was low and the shadows had grown long. We must have looked pitiful: three of us covered in dust, our uniforms wrinkled and sticky with sweat. In the distance, I could see Mama Doray, waiting by the gate, arms crossed. As we got closer, I could make out her unmistakable expression, a mix of relief and fury. My heart sank.

I tried to muster a smile, but before I could say a word, she marched toward us.

"Where have you been?" she demanded, her voice slicing through the stillness of early evening. Without waiting for an answer, she grabbed my ear and twisted, her fingers pinching tight as she scolded me all the way to the front door.

"You think you can just skip the bus and walk home in this heat? What if something happened to you?"

"Ouch, Mama! We're fine! We just—" I began, but she gave my ear another sharp pinch.

"Don't 'ouch' me! You could've been hurt—or worse! You're supposed to take the bus!"

I knew better than to argue. Jun and Mits stood behind me, silent, their faces a mix of guilt and exhaustion. Jun glanced at me, his eyes apologetic—but I caught a flicker of amusement there too. He knew we'd gotten away with something, but just barely.

After a long lecture and a few more pinches, Mama finally let us go. She sent us to wash up, and as I splashed cool water over my face, I couldn't help but grin. Sure, it had been a long walk, and yes, we got in trouble—but for that brief moment in the afternoon, sipping Pepsi and eating cookies, we had a taste of youthful freedom. And that was worth every step and every pinch.

32 Noli Me Tángere

It was another boring Saturday night for me. The night air was thick and heavy, smelling of diesel and moist earth, a familiar Manila perfume. From my window, I watched a small group of neighborhood girls my age, walking down the street. Unlike me, they were enjoying this weekend evening, their laughter like bells chiming in the humid dusk, their bright floral skirts a flash of color against the grimy street. They were probably heading to a Saturday night dance, a world away from my quiet room where I was meant to be reading a book or doing homework. A knot of resentment tightened in my chest. They got to dance, to laugh, to hang out with boys. I, on the other hand, was a prisoner in my home, waiting for a life that felt like it was passing me by.

Even before the war, Mama Doray kept me sheltered, not allowing me to play with other kids in the neighborhood and insisting that I come directly home after school. But all that changed during the occupation. The old rules went out the window. I freely roamed the dangerous streets of our war-torn city, foraged for food, bartered in the black market—I helped us survive. You'd think that would earn me some freedom. But not long after the liberation, the old rules returned. I wanted to speak up—but what could I possibly say? That I was tired of being treated like a child? My resentment had been building for so long that I thought, maybe this time, I could summon the courage to challenge Mama Doray. But, as always, the words caught in my throat, and I ended up backing down.

Whenever I felt trapped in Mama Doray's house, my mind drifted to Cebu. The stifling environment of the Peñafiel house stood in stark contrast to Mama Caring's home there. Sure, it was more crowded, and I had to share a room, but it was filled with the joyful chaos of my siblings and my birth mother's easy, forgiving laughter. And most of all, freedom—the kind that came with fiestas, dances, and late-night laughter shared with my sisters and friends.

To be clear, Mama Caring didn't let us wander the town unchecked. She had her rules—curfews, places to avoid, people we were told to steer clear of. And she always insisted that at least one of our brothers chaperone us, which they were more than happy to do, eager to meet girls and join the fun themselves. But even with the rules, there was no feeling of restriction. What lingered instead was her quiet trust in us—a trust that made all the difference.

The silence of the house was suddenly shattered by the insistent ringing of the telephone and immediately I snapped out of my thoughts of life in Cebu. I heard the muffled murmur of Mama Doray's voice from the parlor. Even though it was indistinct, there was agitation in her tone. After a few clipped sentences, she hung up the receiver with a sharp click. She appeared in my doorway, her face set in a tired, familiar mask. "It's your Papa Emilio," she said, her voice irritated. "He's at the bar again. They want someone to fetch him." I knew what that meant.

Papa Emilio, the man who was more of a father to me than my own, was drinking again. He was a kind man, full of stories and warmth, but the war had left a shadow on his soul that the bottom of a bottle seemed to temporarily soothe. That brutal conflict left its mark on all of us, but I sensed that it affected Papa even more. Perhaps it was the feeling of powerlessness—the stripping away of his role as family protector—and the unbearable loss of a daughter that hollowed him out.

I looked at Mama Doray, a look of weariness etched on her face.

"Go," she said, her gaze distant, fixed on some unseen point on the wall. "Bring him home."

I didn't have to ask which bar. I already knew. The same one where he told stories it seemed no one wanted to hear anymore.

I headed out the door and made my way toward the bar. A brief rain shower had just stopped, but the humidity clung to the night air like a damp blanket. Music drifted from a house down the street, growing louder with each step. A party.

The girls I'd seen earlier were there. I recognized their faces but didn't know their names. I kept my eyes forward, though I could feel theirs on me. They knew me—not by name, but as the girl with the strict mother who wouldn't let her talk to anyone.

I imagined their whispers. Were they snobs? Did they think they were better than us? Wasn't her father the one who drank more than he worked?

I quickened my pace.

When I reached the bar, I noticed the door was propped open. I could hear muffled conversations of the regulars emanating from within, voices layering over each other. With slight trepidation, I entered.

An electric fan was blowing in the corner. The bar wasn't that big, and the air inside felt even thicker than outside. The fan seemed useless, just circulating the sticky air around the room.

The bartender noticed me and knew why I was there. Without saying a word, he nodded his head in the direction Papa Emilio was seated. He was at a table not far from the entrance, his back towards me. Seated across from him was Señor Vega, a Spanish man who lived nearby.

Señor Vega, roughly the same age as Papa Emilio, was one of the neighborhood *insulares*, Spaniards born in the Philippines. His family had been in the Philippines since the late 1800's, most of whom were employed by the *Compañía General de Tabacos de Filipinas* (General Tobacco Company of the Philippines). He himself was one of the *inspectores* (foremen) at the tobacco factory.

They were speaking in Spanish. Their conversation was loud, but not quite an argument.

"You just don't understand," Papa Emilio said in an irate voice.

"No you don't understand Emilio," countered Señor Vega, his voice intense. "You could dress like them, talk like them, and act like them—but to them you will always be an *indio!*"

I froze. I'd heard that word before—*indio*—but never with such venom. It was an insult that cut deep.

Papa Emilio continued to protest, but Señor Vega—still seated—turned slightly and waved his hand dismissively, as if brushing him off like dust.

"Damn you, Vega!" Papa Emilio shouted, rising from his seat in a confrontational posture.

Señor Vega didn't flinch and continued to ignore Papa Emilio. It's as if he had witnessed these feigned displays of aggression before. That seemed to infuriate Papa even more. I interceded.

"Papa!"

My voice cracked through the room like a snapped branch. I hadn't meant to shout, but I couldn't let it go on.

All conversation seemed to stop, and eyes were on me.

Papa Emilio turned quickly in my direction, a sheepish look on his face. He seemed genuinely embarrassed that I had witnessed his outburst.

"It's time to come home," I said, my voice betraying the uneasy sadness I felt for him in that moment."

Papa Emilio nodded silently. With his eyes cast down, he walked slowly toward the door, and together we stepped out into the thick night air.

As we made our way back home, I remained close by Papa Emilio's side to steady him. The effects of one too many whiskeys were apparent in his staggering gait.

In a calmer tone, he continued where he left off with Señor Vega, desperately trying to convince himself of his point.

"You see, just like José Rizal, I believe in the intellectual capacity of Filipinos. We're not inferior to the Spanish. But education is the key! Look at me—I went to Ateneo de Manila, just like José Rizal. I speak Spanish just as well as any of them! I speak English, even better than them!"

"Yes Papa," I agreed, nodding my head.

I had heard Papa Emilio speak about the writings of the national hero of the Philippines before. He was well-versed in José Rizal's books and essays, which advocated reforms under Spanish rule and emphasized education as a path to lift Filipinos from oppression. Yet the old colonial class, exemplified by Señor Vega, seemed determined to dismiss Papa Emilio's vision inspired by Rizal. Though the Spanish and Americans no longer ruled and the Philippines had gained independence, they insisted it made no difference: the country would forever dwell in the shadow of its former colonizers, and the fate of its people would always be measured by the color of their skin.

As we walked home, Papa continued his monologue, occasionally jabbing the air with his finger to emphasize a point. When we arrived, the house was silent; everyone, even Mama Doray, was asleep.

Exhausted from the evening's events, Papa Emilio removed his shoes and reclined on the sofa, the place where he usually slept after returning from the bar.

"Good night, Papa," I said. But he didn't hear me; he had already dozed off, snoring lightly. I stood there for a moment, listening to the rhythmic rumble of his slumber. The man who had once taught me to be proud now slept like a child, worn down by the ghosts that had haunted him his entire life.

As I lay in bed that evening, I thought about my current life with the Peñafiel family. As much as I loved Mama Doray and Papa Emilio, my life with them now just didn't seem the same. I thought coming back would be a return to my old life, but I started realizing that I couldn't go back to how things were before. None of us could.

I also thought about Papa Emilio's fervent belief in education as the path to rising above, a belief rooted in his devotion to the very ideals José Rizal had lived and died for. The pursuit of higher learning, even as practiced by Rizal, went beyond the physical walls of any institution. It meant experiencing life—stumbling sometimes, but growing stronger with each fall. That evening I realized that I couldn't truly grow as a person living under the suffocating governance of Mama Doray, as well meaning as she was. It was time to return to Cebu. To the noise, the laughter, the freedom—and maybe, to myself.

33 Movie Night

When I returned to Cebu, it wasn't with fanfare. I was the prodigal daughter, but unlike in the biblical tale, there was no welcome-home party. I knew I didn't deserve one—and I didn't expect it. Still, even without a celebration, it felt like a homecoming all the same. The moment I stepped through the front door, the house seemed to inhale and exhale around me, as if it had been holding its breath for my return.

The place was still bursting at the seams with life. Along with my siblings, Mama Caring's home now included some of my cousins who were attending a local college. I didn't mind the crowd this time. I found comfort in the noise—the mix of familiar and unfamiliar voices, the near-constant patter of bare footsteps throughout the house, and the clatter of utensils and pots from the kitchen. The entire house seemed alive.

Mama Caring didn't waste time getting me re-enrolled in school. Instead of a Catholic school, like in Manila, I attended Sikatuna Elementary, together with some of my younger siblings. It was a humbling experience. I was placed a few grades behind, and I knew I had a lot of catching up to do. My handwriting was a work in progress, my reading skills needed a lot of improvement, and I struggled with math that my peers seemed to breeze through. Still, I worked hard to keep up. I copied notes until my fingers cramped, tackled extra reading assignments, and asked Benjie and Penang—both excellent students—to tutor me in math after school. I pushed myself, and eventually, it paid off.

But being back home in Cebu wasn't all work and no play. I now had the freedom to spend time with people my own age and enjoy the company of my siblings. I loved exploring my surroundings without the constant vigilance of Mama Doray—it felt like breathing freely for the first time in years. That sense of liberation was intoxicating, like sunlight after a long rain.

One of my favorite weekend rituals was wandering Colon Street with my brothers Nene and Benjie. We'd weave through the crowds, duck into shops, and explore backstreets and alleyways, soaking in the pulse of the city. Colon wasn't just a street—it was Cebu's beating heart.

I didn't know it then, but the area we walked through was steeped in Cebu's history. Colon Street is often called the oldest national road in the Philippines. Named after Cristóbal Colón (the Spanish name for explorer Christopher Columbus), the street's history is deeply intertwined with the Spanish colonial period. In the years leading up to World War II, Colon Street was the undisputed commercial and social hub of Cebu City, its streets lined with fashionable shops, business offices, and movie theaters.

Unfortunately, much of this historical fabric was destroyed during the Battle of Cebu in 1945. When American and Filipino forces landed in Talisay and advanced toward Cebu City, they found it already in ruins. Japanese troops, retreating, set fire to buildings, and American shelling only added to the devastation. Colon Street, once so full of life, was reduced to rubble.

Like other Filipinos across the islands, Cebuanos immediately began rebuilding their beloved city after the war. Post-war rebuilding on Colon Street resulted in the less formal, more utilitarian commercial landscape that defines the area today, with smaller shops and stalls rising from the ashes of the old, elegant thoroughfare.

Of course, our favorite part of Colon Street wasn't the shops or the history—it was the Vision Theater. Marquee posters at the Vision Theater displayed movie stars in bold poses, promising a world beyond our simple lives. Inside the theater, laughter and gasps echoed as the flickering black-and-white scenes transported people to lands and lives they could only dream of. It was the hottest ticket in town, and for kids like us, it was also just out of reach. But we had a plan.

The Vision Theater still bore its war scars, the most notable of which was a small hole on the side of the building. Though some locals had made it worse by chipping away concrete to scavenge steel rods, management had fastened wooden boards to block it. Fortunately for us, the boards didn't cover the hole completely, leaving a narrow slit through which we could see the movie screen inside. The opening wasn't wide enough for all of us, so we took turns, each waiting eagerly for our moment to peer inside.

As we reached the theater, the smell of roasted peanuts and street food drifted through the air, mingling with the excitement of moviegoers. We casually loitered around the front of the theater, checking out the marquee poster to see what was playing. We had to be careful not to attract too much attention, especially from the ticket seller, *Mang* Dolfo, a grumpy old man with a permanent scowl and a cigarette that never seemed to burn out. He sat hunched on his stool at the booth, squinting at us like we were up to no good—which, to be fair, we usually were. He knew us well. We were notorious in his eyes—not for buying tickets, but for finding creative ways to enjoy the show.

"Hey! What are you doing here again?" he barked as we lingered too close to the entrance, pretending to admire the movie posters. We shuffled our feet, feigning innocence. He shook his head, muttering something about kids and mischief.

We played it cool, wandering a few steps away, out of Mang Dolfo's view, but we weren't going anywhere. Nene was the first to make it to our private viewing portal. We took turns—each of us with only a few minutes to watch. The rest of the time was spent crouched down, eager for our turn and trying not to laugh at how absurd we must've looked.

After Nene, it was my turn. I pressed my face to the warm wall, squinting into the theater. A dramatic scene unfolded—a young woman in a flowy dress, her face framed by sorrow, speaking tearfully to a man I couldn't fully make out. Her dress shimmered faintly in the projector's glow, and though I couldn't make out all of her words, her sorrow was unmistakable. Just as it was getting good, Benjie nudged me, signalling the end of my turn. I crawled back, smiling.

When it was Benjie's turn, he grumbled. "I hope I didn't miss any good parts," he muttered. I knew the feeling all too well—the fear of missing the most exciting part. But this was our ritual. We each got our share of pieces, and when the movie ended, we would huddle together, trying to piece the whole story together like a jigsaw puzzle.

Later, outside the theater, standing in front of the marquee poster, with the warm evening breeze tousling our hair, we began the real fun—reconstructing the movie.

"Nene, what happened after the woman cried?" I asked eagerly. "Well, the man—I think he was her husband—grabbed her hand, but he looked angry," Nene explained, his hands mimicking the intensity of the scene.

"No, no," Benjie interrupted, "He wasn't angry! He was scared because there was another guy, the one with the hat, hiding behind the door!"

They went back and forth, animatedly filling in the gaps, their voices overlapping as we tried to recreate the movie. I chimed in with my bit, and soon, we had something resembling a full narrative—well almost.

"Ah, stop it with your blabbering!" Mang Dolfo's voice rang out, startling us from our huddle. He'd heard our little movie retelling and, like clockwork, was ready to shoo us away. "You'll spoil it for the paying customers!" he grumbled, waving his hand in mock frustration.

We ran off laughing, our flip-flops slapping against the pavement, knowing we'd be back next weekend to do it all over again.

Though we couldn't afford to step inside the theater, we carried those moments with us. In our own way, we had watched the movie, felt its drama, and lived through its highs and lows together. It didn't matter that our version was always a little disjointed, a little out of order. If anything, that's what made it ours.

34 Glimpse Into The Unknown

The streets were alive with laughter, music, and the smell of lechon roasting on the spit. When the carnival came to town, it was as if the whole place breathed a different air—one thick with excitement and celebration. The *perya*, our small-town fair that always arrived with the fiestas, was something everyone looked forward to. With its small Ferris wheel (*ruweda*), carousel (*tsubibo*), betting games, and food stalls, there was something for young and old to enjoy.

Most people came for the rides and the food, but I loved these fiestas for another reason—they brought my family together again. After the long years of war that had kept us apart, every shared laugh and simple meal felt like a piece of our lives stitched back in place.

That year, I went with my sisters Helen and Penang. We wove our way through the crowded plaza, our dresses swirling with the breeze, the fabric clinging to our legs in the afternoon heat. The whole town was buzzing. Children darted between the colorful stalls, women fanned themselves under the shade of makeshift tents, and men clustered around the gambling booths. None of these things interested my sisters, though. They couldn't stop talking about one thing—the fortune teller.

"She's here again this year," Penang whispered as we walked, her voice low and excited. "And everyone says she can really see the future."

I couldn't help but laugh—Penang, of all people, believing in fortune tellers? She was the studious one, grounded in logic and common sense.

"You don't really believe in that stuff, do you?" I asked.

"I don't know," she said, smiling. "It could be interesting. Just for fun."

Helen, my happy-go-lucky older sister, chimed in. "It does sound like fun. Maybe we should check it out."

I smiled at their enthusiasm, though I had no real interest in seeing the fortune teller. What was the point? What could she tell me that I didn't already know? My future felt ordinary, predictable—marriage, children, a life built around the familiar streets of Cebu. My world seemed small then, and I had no reason to believe it would ever grow beyond what I could see.

Still, Helen and Penang were persistent. After weaving through the crowd, they found the small, dimly lit stall. The air inside smelled faintly of candles and dried herbs. The fortune teller sat waiting, her wrinkled hands resting lightly on a worn wooden table. Her eyes, dark and sharp, seemed to see everything—and nothing—all at once.

"We'd like our fortunes read, *Manang*," Helen said eagerly, plunking a few coins onto the table. The fortune teller nodded and took the money without a word.

Penang went first, her voice bright with anticipation. The woman spoke of long life, a happy family, many children. Penang beamed, nodding at every word as if her future were already unfolding before her.

Next was Helen. She held her breath as the fortune teller described a husband who would love her fiercely, who would make her laugh even when she didn't want to. And again—children, a home full of laughter. Helen listened, smiling, already convinced.

I stood a few feet away, pretending to study the nearby stalls, but my attention kept drifting back to the table. It was almost amusing, the way they took it all so seriously.

"Your turn," Penang said, turning to me.

I shook my head. "No, thanks. You know I don't believe in that."

The fortune teller's eyes flicked up to me, and a shiver ran down my spine. There was something unsettling about her gaze. "Come," she said softly. "No charge. Just to see."

I hesitated, but Helen and Penang were already tugging at my arms. "Come on, just for fun," Helen said. "What's the harm?"

Reluctantly, I sat. The fortune teller took my hands in hers—cool and dry, like paper. She studied my palms for what felt like an eternity before speaking.

"You will live a long life," she said at last, her voice low and rhythmic. "A prosperous life."

I let out a small breath. At least it wasn't anything strange. Prosperity I could accept.

But then she added, "You will travel to many foreign lands, places you've never heard of—far across the oceans."

I blinked. Foreign lands? That made no sense. I'd never been farther than Manila and had no plans to go anywhere.

"I don't know about that," I murmured.

The woman didn't answer, only traced the lines on my palms as if searching for something hidden. "There will be challenges," she said at last, her tone deepening. "But you will overcome them."

"And what about love?" I asked lightly, half teasing, half curious.

For the first time, she faltered. Her fingers paused. She looked up, then quickly away. "Love..." she said slowly. "Love will come—but it is not for me to say how or when."

I frowned. "What does that mean?"

The fortune teller released my hands, her expression unreadable. "You will see," she said softly. "In time, you will see."

A strange flutter rose in my chest as I stood. Her words lingered, though I couldn't say why. My sisters, however, were glowing.

"She said you'll travel to foreign lands!" Helen exclaimed, nudging me. "Imagine that!"

"Maybe you'll meet someone there," Penang teased.

I laughed it off, but her words stayed with me. Foreign lands. Love that would come in its own time.

As we walked away, the laughter and music of the carnival washed over us again, bright and familiar. Yet something inside me had shifted—a quiet awareness that perhaps my life might stretch farther than the streets I knew.

35 New Beginnings

The bells of the University of San Carlos still rang in my ears long after the ceremony ended. I had walked across the stage for my high school graduation and taken my diploma with trembling fingers. On the way back to my seat, still in a mild trance from the moment, I nearly tripped as the sound of clapping and cheers echoed from my family and friends.

My journey to that moment had not been easy. After falling behind a few grades during the war, I had struggled to catch up, studying late into the night under the weak glow of the bulb in our living room. But I did it. Standing there in my cap and gown, the stiff fabric clinging in the afternoon heat, I felt a lump rise in my throat. For the first time in a long while, I allowed myself to feel proud.

Mama Doray and Papa Emilio had always urged me to reach a little farther, to make my own way. Finishing school was just the beginning.

After graduation, I could hardly keep still, my thoughts racing toward what lay ahead. I wanted a job—a good one—where I could wear heels and pencil skirts like the women in the magazines, a job that would let me stretch my wings in this growing, restless city. Cebu was changing fast, and I wanted to change with it—not just wait for life to happen, but step out and meet it.

A few weeks after graduation, Tia Carmen, Papa Peping's older sister, paid us a visit. She arrived with a sort of secret glow, settling at the table with a dramatic sigh before lifting her eyebrows at me, eyes twinkling.

"Ging, I have a friend who works at PLDT," she began, her voice carrying a note of suspense, "and they're looking for an operator—someone who speaks all the languages, just like you."

A rush of excitement prickled up my spine. PLDT! The Philippine Long Distance Telephone Company, right here in Cebu! I could hardly believe it. I knew its importance—how it connected families, friends, and businesses across islands and oceans. If I could work there, I'd be more than just a girl fresh out of high school; I'd be part of something much larger, something that connected the islands in ways only those big black wires could.

"Tagalog, Visayan, Spanish, and English. They specifically want someone who knows them all," Tia continued, nodding knowingly. "I told my friend you'd be perfect."

The next day, I polished my shoes and tucked my hair neatly into a low bun, just as I had seen the seasoned working women do. My skirt was crisp, my blouse perfectly ironed, each crease in place, each button fastened. Nervous excitement bubbled in my stomach as I walked to the PLDT office.

Inside, the call center office hummed with activity—rows of desks and switchboards, women in headsets, voices blending together in a steady rhythm. I met Señora Velasquez, Tia's friend, who ran the office with calm authority.

The interview was brief. Señora Velasquez focused on my languages, asking me to switch between them while talking about school, family, and even the weather. I responded with confidence in each, my words flowing seamlessly. When I mentioned my studies at San Carlos, she nodded approvingly, eyebrows lifting just slightly.

"Well, señorita," she said, smiling warmly, "I think you'll do just fine here. When can you start?"

The job, Señora Velasquez explained, was challenging. It required focus, speed, and precision. But there was room to grow. As she described the daily duties, possible promotions, and the stability of the position, I could practically feel my future unfolding right there in her office.

My first day arrived swiftly. I immediately began learning the ropes and was amazed at how quickly I picked it up. Before long, I was flying solo! I sat at one of the switchboards and donned my headset. An electric surge pulsed through me as my fingers danced over the plugs and buttons. Calls came in every few seconds—Tagalog, Visayan, Spanish, English. I greeted each caller with a smile in my voice, connecting people across towns, cities, islands. The rhythm of the clicks and beeps became a steady heartbeat to my day, a soundtrack that seemed to reverberate in sync with the city itself.

By the end of each shift, I felt a rush of satisfaction—tired, yes, but proud. My family couldn't contain their excitement. Papa told everyone in the neighborhood about my new job, while Mama bragged about her daughter's success to friends at the market. I knew what a privilege it was to have this work, how few young women in our time could claim their own income and independence.

I began to see how language—the simple act of knowing how to speak to others—was a rare gift, one that made me useful in ways I hadn't imagined. Each call was a tiny adventure: someone seeking help, directions, or just a familiar voice to bridge the distance between them and their loved ones. In a way, I was weaving people together, literally at my fingertips.

Every paycheck brought a small thrill—not because I wanted to spend it, but because I knew exactly what I would do with it. I had always been frugal. Even as a young woman, I never cared much for fancy clothes, perfumes, or the newest shades of lipstick my coworkers gossiped about. Instead, I saved, each peso carefully set aside like a tiny brick in a house I could not yet see but somehow knew was waiting for me.

I'd inherited my money-minded ways from my older Peñafiel sister, Carlota. She had been my quiet role model, guiding me without realizing it. Carlota was a trailblazer in her own right, having started work at the San Miguel Brewery long before I'd finished school. I remember watching her carefully portion her salary, setting some aside for our family, a bit for herself, and, with a spark in her eye, a small part for "the future."

Carlota had a fascination with investing—an unusual trait, especially for a young woman in our time. She'd learned about it from an older coworker who spoke of shares and dividends with a quiet confidence. Over the years, she set aside any extra pesos to buy small shares in San Miguel. Her modest investments gradually grew into a nest egg she could rely on. She called it her "secret weapon," a discreet way to claim her independence and secure her future.

Her approach made a lasting impression on me. While other girls saved for new dresses, Carlota was carefully building her future with every peso she tucked away in stocks. She first introduced me to the idea that wealth wasn't just money in the bank, but something that could grow if planted and nurtured. I watched her choices with fascination and a growing resolve to do the same.

Once I'd settled into my job at PLDT, I followed her lead. Every payday, I took care of my expenses and set a little aside for my family, as she had done. The rest went into my "secret weapon"—for me, PLDT shares. Each share I bought made me feel more secure—not for wealth, but for having something of my own, a foundation I could rely on.

With my portfolio steadily growing, I began to consider bigger steps. One quiet, thoughtful evening, I made a decision that would shape my life and my family's future: I would buy a plot of land in Sun Valley, a quiet area of Cebu just beginning to develop. It was an ambitious move, but one I was ready for.

The property wasn't much to look at back then—a modest plot of green that needed clearing and tending. But it was mine. I gradually poured my savings into the land, and eventually, a sturdy house rose from the soil—a testament to every long night, every saved peso, and every wise word from my sister. Every visit, I imagined the home I would build and the roots I would lay down.

Today, that house still stands in Sun Valley, filled with laughter, children's footsteps, and the smell of home-cooked meals. My relatives live there now, enjoying the fruits of decisions I made as a young woman full of dreams. Looking back, I realize that each choice, each small step, was part of a path I'd crafted not just for myself, but for everyone who would come after me. My life might not have glittered with perfumes, expensive clothes, or luxuries, but it was rich in something far more enduring: a legacy built on savings, investments, and the quiet confidence of a young woman who had dared to believe in her own future.

36 Dance Hall Days

I'd been working at PLDT for almost a year, and life was good. Though I still lived at home, I felt a growing sense of independence and was beginning to embrace adulthood on my own terms. On this particular Friday night, after a long workweek, I was ready to indulge in one of my favorite activities: meeting up with friends at a dance party. The air buzzed with the promise of music, laughter, and the thrill of something new. I could already hear the rhythms spilling from the record player—the quick steps of the jive and mambo, the lazy drawl of a slow waltz. The world felt wide open, as if I could breathe in the freedom of it all.

My sister Penang and I were no longer teenagers and didn't have to ask for permission to go out, but we were still respectful enough to our mother to let her know we had plans for the evening. In the past, our older brother Julio would accompany us, just to make sure we were "safe." The truth was, he also wanted an excuse to go out and dance with some of our friends. We didn't really need a bodyguard following us around but since Julio didn't interfere in our mingling and dancing, we didn't object.

That afternoon, as we were getting ready, Julio and our other brother Carlos came home and slumped on the sofa in the living room. Both of them were exhausted from their shift at the San Miguel bottling plant. I was adjusting the strap of my dress, imagining the way it would move with me as I danced. Julio, his face and shirt damp with sweat, looked at us and shook his head.

"I'm too tired to chaperone you girls tonight," he said, rubbing his eyes. "So, you can't go."

The words hit me like a slap. I stopped fiddling with my dress and stared at him. "What do you mean we can't go?" I asked, my voice shaking with disbelief.

"You heard me. I said no. I'm not coming with you, and you're not going out without me," he said, leaning back on the sofa as if that was the final word.

But I wasn't a child anymore, and I wasn't going to let him—or anyone—tell me what I could or couldn't do. Not anymore. The strict world I had grown up in, where every move had to be approved and every smile monitored, was behind me now. I wasn't going to miss the night, not after spending all week looking forward to it.

"I'm going," I said, louder now. "With or without you."

I saw his eyes snap open. He stood up, slow and deliberate, his face hardening into a look I knew too well. It was the look of someone who wasn't going to let me get away with anything. But I wasn't scared. My heart raced, but I wouldn't back down.

"What did you say?" he growled, taking a deliberate step closer.

"I said, I'm going out," I repeated, standing my ground. "I don't care if you're too tired. I'm not a little girl anymore."

Before I could blink, he was in front of me, his right index finger pointing directly at my face.

"How dare you disrespect me! I'm your older brother—you'll do as I say!" he shouted, his tone leaving no doubt.

Though Penang wanted to go out too, she didn't want to have a confrontation with Julio.

"Come on Ging. It's okay, I don't feel like dancing tonight. Let's just stay home and listen to music here." She took hold of my hand and started to pull me away, but I let go and stepped back.

"No! I'm going dancing tonight and nobody is going to stop me!"

All of a sudden Julio grabbed me by the shoulders, his grip firm but not painful. My sister let out a small gasp, startled by the rising tension of the situation. He leaned in closer, his face inches from mine, and yelled, "You're nothing but a spoiled brat! Is this how the Peñafiels raised you?"

I saw the anger burning in his eyes, but I wasn't about to back down. I glared back at him in silent defiance.

Carlos then stepped in, resting a hand on Julio's shoulder as if to hold him back before things got out of hand.

"Julio, what's the big deal? Just let the girls go."

Julio shrugged him off and stepped back. "You're too stubborn for your own good," he said with a smirk.

I exhaled, rolling my eyes at him, though I couldn't suppress the grin tugging at the corner of my lips. Julio liked to play the tough guy, but we both knew he wasn't really going to stop me.

As he sat back down, shaking his head in mock frustration, I grabbed Penang's hand and headed for the door. Julio was still fuming, but I didn't care. "Don't wait up," I called over my shoulder, half-laughing, half-mocking.

The cool night air hit me the moment we stepped outside, sending a rush of excitement through me. The sound of lively music drifted from the house party in the distance, beckoning us closer. My heart quickened with every step we took.

And as we made our way down the street, I couldn't help but smile. Tonight, I was free—free from the walls that had once held me in, free from the rules that had tried to keep me small. For the first time, I was dancing to my own rhythm—and I wasn't going to let anything, or anyone, stop me.

37 Orlando

It was Felix, my brother-in-law, who first introduced me to Orlando. Felix, Helen's husband, managed a local movie theater downtown—a job he took great pride in. For years, he'd helped bring a bit of joy and Hollywood glamour to Cebu, showing the latest films from Manila and beyond. He loved his work, and because of that, he was always rubbing elbows with the men behind the scenes—the ones who ferried the films to the island. That's how he knew Orlando.

Orlando worked for the distribution company responsible for getting new releases to theaters across Cebu. Felix liked to joke that Orlando was the man who "brought Hollywood to the islands," though in truth, he was more of a quiet cog in the machine than anything glamorous. Orlando wasn't the sort who announced himself when he entered a room. He was the opposite of Felix, whose booming laugh could fill an entire lobby. Orlando slipped in and out of places quietly, a stack of film reels under his arm and a polite nod for whoever crossed his path.

The night we met, Felix brought him over after work. It was one of those sticky, humid evenings when the air felt thick. These were the days before air conditioning was common in Filipino homes. We had a few electric fans running, but they didn't seem to help much. Helen and I were setting the table when Felix came in with Orlando trailing behind, looking slightly uncomfortable in his neatly pressed shirt and tie. Felix, as usual, was in the middle of some story that had him grinning ear to ear, while Orlando stood back, hands in his pockets, glancing around the room as if unsure whether to stay or leave.

"Meet Orlando," Felix announced, clapping a hand on his shoulder. "He's the one who makes sure I get all those films on time—so we've got him to thank for our Saturday night entertainment!"

Orlando gave a shy smile, more out of politeness than amusement. "It's really not much," he said quietly. "Just logistics, mostly."

Felix wouldn't let him off so easily. "Not much? Ha! If it weren't for you, we'd be stuck watching the same old movies again and again. You keep Cebu up to date, my friend!"

I remember watching Orlando as he shifted from foot to foot, clearly uncomfortable with the praise. He was good-looking in that understated way I would later come to recognize—tall (for a Filipino), slightly stooped, as if he'd spent too much time bent over paperwork. His hair was neatly combed, though a few strands had fallen into his eyes. He wore that faint, thoughtful expression I would come to know well, as if his mind was half somewhere else. At that moment, he looked up and caught my eye, offering me a small, awkward nod.

Felix, never one for subtlety, gave him a nudge. "This is my sister-in-law, Ging. She's smart and has a good job at PLDT." His voice filled the room, but I could see Orlando's eyes flicker with discomfort, as if unsure how to respond to such exuberance.

"Nice to meet you," he said softly, almost hesitant. He was polite, respectful—the way men were expected to be when meeting a young woman for the first time.

We exchanged the usual pleasantries, though it was clear from the start that Orlando wasn't one for small talk. Unlike Felix, who could charm anyone with a laugh, Orlando's words were measured, deliberate, a little too serious. I could tell he cared about his work—how the reels arrived by boat from Manila, how carefully they handled the nitrate film to keep it from catching fire. I admired his attention to detail, but part of me found it all so... dry. I was young then, drawn to liveliness and laughter. I didn't yet understand that there was a quiet kind of steadiness in men like Orlando, the kind that doesn't call attention to itself but lingers—long after the noise has faded.

In any case, Felix liked him well enough and began bringing him by the house every few weeks after that. Orlando was always polite, always on time, always wearing that same neatly pressed shirt and tie, even when the heat made everyone else loosen their collars. I started to notice the way his eyes lit up whenever he talked about films—though not the films themselves, really, but the logistics behind getting them from one place to another. He was a man who valued order, precision, routine. There was comfort in that, I suppose, though it wasn't the kind of comfort that stirred anything in me.

But Felix saw something else. He started dropping hints—little comments about how Orlando was a "steady young man from a good family," or how he was "going places in the company." Felix was a practical man, and I suppose, in his eyes, Orlando was exactly the kind of man a woman should marry. Reliable, stable, church-going. A man who wouldn't give you trouble, who'd come home every night at the same time, sit down for dinner, and ask about your day.

And so, little by little, it was arranged. Orlando never courted me in the traditional sense—there were no grand gestures, no flowers or late-night serenades. His proposal, sincere as it was, was understated. One evening, as he walked me home from work, we stopped by a park and sat on a bench. Ever the traditionalist, he dropped to one knee and offered me a ring. I wasn't surprised; I had expected it would come someday, sooner rather than later. So I accepted.

After our engagement, we settled into a kind of routine. He would walk me home after church on Sundays and ask me about my week.

Our conversations were always the same: the weather, how things were going at PLDT, how Felix was doing at the theater. I found myself answering on autopilot, offering the same replies each week, until it felt like we were stuck in a loop of politeness. It wasn't unpleasant. Orlando was kind and earnest, and I knew he cared for me deeply. I wanted to return that feeling, but mine never seemed to grow past affection. In those days, that was enough reason to say yes—or at least, it was supposed to be.

38 The Signs

If my misgivings about Orlando were subdued, Papa Emilio's were the total opposite. He was blunt in his assessment after they first met. During one of his business trips to Cebu after our engagement, I introduced them over lunch. Orlando, knowing how close I was to Papa Emilio, wanted to make a good impression. But his nervousness and lack of conversational skills made it difficult. He was so flustered he even struggled to discuss something he was passionate about—his work. After about an hour, he looked at his watch and politely excused himself, citing a business obligation. I'm sure he was relieved to leave the restaurant.

Papa Emilio was cordial and polite during their meeting, but as soon as Orlando left, he shared his true feelings.

"He's not the right one for you, Ging," he started. "He's too boring."

"But Papa, he's a really nice guy. He comes from a good family and has a good job." I almost felt like I was trying to convince myself, not just Papa Emilio.

"Good job? Doing what—running a movie projector?"

"He works distributing the films, Papa," I explained. "And… he loves me."

"But do you love him?" Papa asked.

He noticed my hesitation and placed his hand on mine.

"Look, mija, you don't need to rush into marriage. Especially if he's not the right one for you. When the right man comes along, you'll know."

Papa Emilio's words stuck with me and made me doubt getting married to Orlando even more.

But he wasn't the only one sowing seeds of doubt about marriage. There was someone at work too.

Erlinda was one of the seasoned operators at PLDT. In her mid-thirties, she was born and raised in Cebu. Like me, she had a Spanish father and a Filipina mother. We never really talked about personal matters, although I knew she was married and had kids, and I'd heard in passing that she had lost family in the war.

One afternoon we happened to be in the break room at the same time, both eating lunch.

"Hi, Ging! How's your shift going so far?" she asked.

"Nothing exciting so far," I replied. "How about you?"

"About the same. Hopefully it changes, otherwise I'm afraid I'll fall asleep at the switchboard," she said with a teasing laugh.

"So, I heard you're getting married," Erlinda said, changing the topic.

"Oh yes, in the spring. My fiancé's name is Orlando. He works for a film distribution company," I told her.

"How old are you?" she asked.

"Nineteen, but I'll be twenty this year," I replied.

"Ay, niña… so young," she said, shaking her head slightly.

"Do you want to get married?" she asked.

I was taken aback, not expecting such a direct question.

"Uh, why yes, of course," I replied unconvincingly.

Like Papa Emilio, Erlinda noticed the hesitation in my voice.

"Can I give you a little advice, niña?" she started.

I nodded quietly.

"You have your whole life ahead of you. You're so young. Enjoy your life while you're young. Don't rush into marriage. If he loves you, he'll wait. If not… you're a pretty girl, you won't have a hard time finding a man," she said with a wink.

Erlinda patted my hand and went back to her lunch. Her words lingered with me long after she left, echoing Papa Emilio's caution and stirring more doubts about my engagement.

Even after hearing the advice from Papa Emilio and Erlinda, I was still undecided. Orlando was polite, well-liked, and had a good job. By every measure, he was a good catch. But even as our marriage became more inevitable, I couldn't shake the feeling that something was missing. There was no fire, no spark of excitement—but was that reason enough to call it off?

I prayed for a sign from God to help me make the right decision. And my prayer was answered. Not with one sign, but two.

One evening after my shift, Orlando came to walk me home. I saw immediately that something was troubling him—something he didn't quite know how to say.

"What's wrong?" I asked.

"You know my older brother Antonio, the one who lives in Manila?"

I nodded.

"Well, I just found out he's getting married too, and he's planned his wedding for this year. It's bad luck! We have to reschedule."

The bad luck Orlando was referring to is the Filipino superstition *sukob*. The belief is that two siblings should not marry within the same calendar year, as it is said to bring misfortune to one or both couples—sickness, financial hardship, even death.

I wasn't especially superstitious, but I didn't have any desire to invite bad luck into a marriage I was already doubting. Besides, it would give me more time to decide if Orlando was truly the one. So, we agreed to move our wedding to the following spring.

Then, that January, a massive typhoon struck the islands. Orlando's parents' home was practically destroyed. The cost of rebuilding would be steep; a wedding and reception would simply be too much.

"My love, we'll have to postpone our wedding again—to next

year," Orlando said gently, taking my hands in his.

That's when I knew. My marriage to Orlando was not meant to be.

Still holding his hands, I looked up at him. "I have to be honest with you. You've been nothing but kind and loving to me, and I owe you that much."

Sensing what was coming next, a look of sadness crossed his face.

"I've been having doubts about getting married for some time," I admitted. "And these postponements—two of them now—maybe they're signs. I just don't know, Orlando. Maybe we weren't right for each other."

He nodded silently. Words weren't necessary—I could see the hurt in his eyes.

Orlando gave my hands a gentle squeeze, pulled me into a tight embrace, and held me for a few moments.

A wave of emotions hit me. Was I making the right decision? Was I being too hasty in letting go of Orlando?

When he finally released me, Orlando stepped back and took one last look. He gazed into my eyes and smiled. Then he leaned in and gently kissed me on the cheek. And with that, he turned and walked down the street, disappearing into the darkened horizon.

I continued staring into the distance even after Orlando left. Then I started to cry. Wasn't I supposed to feel relieved that I was getting out of a marriage I didn't want? Wasn't I supposed to feel happy that I wasn't going to be tied down at a young age?

But I didn't feel relieved or happy. Instead, I felt sadness—sadness from a loss I couldn't truly comprehend.

39 City Lights

A couple of weeks had passed since I broke off my engagement with Orlando. His departure still stung, but the ache no longer ruled my days. At first, it was difficult even to get out of bed and go to work. But little by little, I felt something stir inside me—an inner voice urging me not to let life pass me by. I ignored it at first, preferring to wallow in sorrow and self-pity. Then I thought back to Erlinda's advice: to enjoy my youthful, single life. It was as if I could hear her saying, "You've cried enough, Ging. It's time to dance again."

My friends from work, Lourdes and Dolly, were happy to hear that I was ready to get back into the social scene. We were all about the same age and had started spending time together soon after I began working at PLDT. Like me, they loved to dance—always ready to swing, foxtrot, or cha-cha at parties or informal get-togethers. Even while I was engaged to Orlando, I'd occasionally go out with them, but with his two left feet, he never felt comfortable joining us. Eventually, I stopped going altogether, spending quiet Friday and Saturday nights with Orlando instead.

My first taste of freedom as a single young woman came at a dance party hosted by one of Lourdes's cousins. Her cousin's house had a large covered courtyard, perfect for mingling and moving to the music. Lourdes told me I'd see a lot of familiar faces, as well as some new ones—young people my age visiting from college.

"Who knows? You might meet someone new!" she teased, her eyes glinting.

I laughed. I wasn't looking to meet anyone, really. I just wanted to feel joy again—to move, to laugh, to stop being the girl who spent her Saturdays hiding from the world.

When the three of us arrived at the party, we were immediately greeted by Lourdes's cousin, Cory. She welcomed us warmly, pointed out the table with snacks and refreshments, and told us to have a good time before returning to her guests. A record player in the corner filled the courtyard with popular dance music, and several couples were already spinning in the center of the floor. The atmosphere was festive, the kind that made you smile without realizing it. I felt myself instinctively swaying to the rhythm.

A small group of our friends spotted us and waved us over. We greeted one another with smiles and hugs, catching up on families and work life. I was relieved that no one asked about Orlando. Being out again—part of the noise and movement of a Saturday night—felt good, really good. It was as if all the sadness from the previous weeks had vanished, as though it had never existed at all. Seeing friends, dancing, laughing—*this* was what Erlinda had meant when she told me to enjoy my youth.

It wasn't long before we started pairing up and getting down to the real business of the evening: dancing.

The guys in our circle of friends were all great dance partners. There were no romantic feelings between them and us girls. To Dolly, Lourdes, and me, they were like brothers—polite, protective, and always fun to be around. And that was fine by me. For me, dancing was simply a way to be with friends and let go of the week's worries. But that evening, there was someone who caught my eye.

His name was Tomas, a friend of a friend from our group. Tall and handsome, he had a smile and wit that could charm anyone in the room. A medical student from a well-to-do Cebu family, Tomas carried himself with quiet confidence. That night he was impeccably dressed, his movements easy, his demeanor self-assured. And he was a very good dancer. Shortly after we were introduced, he asked me out to the floor. I was immediately impressed by his rhythm and poise—his steps were smooth and precise, his touch steady but never intrusive. Most of my guy friends were good dancers, but they sometimes showed traces of boyish awkwardness. Not Tomas.

Between dances, we sat on the sidelines drinking cold Cokes, sharing stories about our families and lives. Unlike Orlando, Tomas spoke with an easy excitement, his words bubbling with energy. And he was good about not just talking about himself. He asked me questions about my work and my family, listening with genuine interest, as if every word I said mattered. He made me feel like the most interesting girl in the world.

Tomas was ambitious, but he didn't come across as arrogant. He told me he wanted to become a doctor because of his lola, who had lost her sight at an early age due to a preventable illness. He admired José Rizal for the same reason—how he had studied medicine to help his own mother.

"I don't think I'll ever be as famous as our national hero," Tomas said with a chuckle, "but you have to start somewhere."

He was unlike any man I had ever met—smart, charming, and seemingly modest. *Is this the kind of man Papa Emilio would approve of?* I wondered.

After several more dances, we took another break to cool off, and that's when he mentioned a special spot in the hills above Cebu.

"You know," Tomas said, leaning closer, "there's a place not far from here where you can see the city lights. It's beautiful, especially on nights like this."

I looked at him, intrigued. The idea of seeing the city from above sounded magical. I had never seen anything like that before.

"Would you like to see it?" he asked. His voice was gentle, but there was something else in his eyes—something that made me pause for a moment. But I was young and naive, and the idea of seeing the city lights—just the two of us—felt too enchanting to resist. So I smiled and said yes.

We got into his car, an old American model, shiny and sleek. Just sitting inside made me feel important. We drove out of town, the road growing darker as we left the lively streets behind. I told myself this was safe. After all, Tomas was a gentleman, wasn't he?

As we approached a secluded spot overlooking the city, he pulled over and turned off the engine. The view was breathtaking—the twinkling lights of Cebu stretched out before us like tiny diamonds on black velvet. I smiled, genuinely delighted, but before I could take it all in, Tomas leaned in closer.

"You're really something special," he murmured, his voice lower now, and I felt his breath on my cheek.

I tensed. His hand touched my arm lightly at first, then slid to my waist. My heart began to race. This wasn't what I had imagined when he offered to show me the city lights.

"I—I think we should go back," I stammered, trying to pull away, but he didn't let go. Instead, he moved closer, his intentions suddenly clear.

"Come on, we're just having a little fun," he said softly, but there was a sharpness in his voice that made me feel cold inside.

I pushed his hand away, panic rising in my chest. "No, please—take me back to the party."

But he persisted, his voice still gentle but now coaxing, pressing. Tears welled in my eyes before I could stop them. I didn't mean to cry, but I was scared, and everything about the moment felt wrong.

With all my strength, I shoved him back. "I said no!" My voice shook, but it was firm. I opened the car door and scrambled out, my legs trembling. "I'll walk back," I said, though I wasn't sure where we even were.

Tomas sighed heavily, his charming mask slipping into frustration. He sat there for a moment, realizing I wasn't going to back down. Then, to my relief, he agreed to take me back.

The drive was silent, the air thick with tension. I stared out the window, wiping away tears, trying to compose myself. I could still see the lights in the distance, but they no longer seemed magical. They reminded me instead of my own naivete that night. When we reached Lourdes's cousin's house, I quickly got out of the car without looking back. Tomas drove away without a word.

Lourdes saw me as soon as I entered the courtyard. She could tell something wasn't right.

"Are you okay? What's wrong?" she asked.

"It's nothing—my stomach's bothering me. I just need some fresh air. If it's okay, I'd like to go home."

"Of course," she said gently. We gathered our things, said our goodbyes, and left.

I never told Lourdes or Dolly what happened that night. I was ashamed of my naivete in accepting Tomas's offer, and I didn't want to spoil our future dance nights together. I still went with them to dances afterward, but I kept my guard up a little more—careful not to let impulsive decisions get the best of me.

That night, before going to bed, I whispered a prayer of thanks for my guardian angel watching over me.

And I thought of Mama Doray's warning from years ago—about men who offer favors only to expect something in return.

Now, I understood.

In the weeks that followed, I threw myself back into my routines—work, family, and quiet evenings at home. The experience with Tomas faded into something distant, yet it left a trace I couldn't quite name. I didn't feel bitter, only wiser, more cautious about the faces people wear in public and the hearts they hide in private. Life moved forward, as it always does, but a small part of me—once so eager to chase the shimmer of city lights—had learned to look for light in safer, truer places.

40 Random Caller

After the incident with Tomas, I swore off men for a while. During that time, the only guys I interacted with were my brothers and the ones in my close-knit dancing group. Since no one knew what had happened, friends and family were always trying to play matchmaker, and I always politely refused. Dating was the furthest thing from my mind, and I wasn't quite ready to meet anyone new. It wasn't resentment or fear, just a quiet fatigue—a need to breathe on my own again. But fate, as it often does, had other plans.

That particular evening was unusually busy for a weeknight. I was at my station, switchboard in front of me: a wall of sockets and blinking lights, cords dangling like thick noodles. With my headset firmly in place, as if fused to the side of my head, I worked through a steady barrage of connections. My hands glided across the panel, performing a kind of dance between fingers, cables, and sockets. Shifts like these could be intense, but they made the hours pass quickly.

As the calls began to slow, I told Dolly I was going to take a break in a few minutes and asked if she could cover for me. She nodded and kept on with her line. I had just finished a call and was about to remove my headset when another one came in. I sighed, settled the headset back in place, and muttered to myself, "All right, one last call."

"Operator, how may I assist you?" I said, repeating a line I'd spoken thousands of times—without realizing that this one would be different.

What greeted me wasn't the usual polite request for a connection. Instead, there came a heavy sigh, followed by a voice that slurred just a little too much.

"Hey... uh, I need to get connected to the Crown Hotel," the man said, practically mumbling from the booze. "Trying to reach a friend."

I tried to suppress an eye roll, glancing at the blinking lights on my board. Great. Another one of those calls. I looked over at Lourdes, who raised an eyebrow. We both had a radar for these types—the men who'd had a little too much to drink and ended up calling for connections they could barely remember.

"Certainly, sir. May I know the room number or the name of the guest?" I asked, keeping my tone even though my patience was wearing thin.

There was a pause, then a deep chuckle on the other end of the line. "No clue about the room number. But his name... his name is Ernesto, Nesto," he drawled.

"Has anyone ever told you that you have a nice voice? What's your name, Miss Operator?"

I stiffened, already regretting I'd taken the call. This wasn't the first time some man tried to flirt over the phone, using the anonymity of the line as a shield. Some men thought telephone operators were easy targets—faceless voices hidden behind the switchboard.

"Sir, I'm afraid I can't give out my personal information," I answered firmly.

"Aw, come on, you could tell me your name. What's the harm in that?" he persisted.

I'd handled plenty like him before—lonely voices looking for amusement on the line.

"My name is Operator 322," I said curtly. "Would you like me to connect you to the front desk?"

"No, no… not yet," he said, sounding more relaxed now. "I'm sure he's there, but let's talk first. Hey, if I tell you my name, will you tell me yours?"

It was starting to get really annoying.

"Sir, I told you, I can't give out my personal—"

"It's Ramon," he interrupted. "My name is Ramon. It's nice to meet you, Miss Operator 322."

What a strange coincidence, I thought. Ramon—the same as my last name.

I tried to regain focus. "Sir, do you want me to connect you to the hotel or not?"

He laughed. "You're a tough one. I like that. You wanna know my last name?"

"Sir, I told you—"

"It's Dormido."

For a moment I thought he was joking. We'd been speaking in Tagalog, so he probably assumed I wouldn't catch the meaning. Many Filipinos had Spanish surnames without knowing what they meant—but I did. Dormido means "asleep."

"Sir, I really need to connect you to the hotel now. If not, I'll have to end this call."

"Okay, okay. Connect me," he sighed, then added quickly, "But only if you promise to meet me. How about coffee sometime, Operator 322?"

I ignored his offer. "Okay, sir—connecting you to the front desk of the Crown Hotel."

And with that, my brief conversation with Ramon was over.

About two hours later, Lourdes received a call. She put her hand over the mouthpiece and gave me a little wave to get my attention.

"Hey, it's for you. I'll patch it through."

Calls asking for a specific operator weren't that unusual, especially if the caller knew your number. I sighed; I had a feeling I knew who it was.

"Operator 322, how may I help you?"

"Hey, Operator 322, it's Ramon."

It was him. I was surprised he hadn't already passed out drinking with his buddies—but he actually sounded more sober this time.

"I'm sorry we got off on the wrong foot," he said. "The truth is, I'm new in town. I work with Philippine Airlines and just got transferred here from Negros. I don't know many people yet, so I'm trying to make new friends."

"Sir, we're not allowed to—"

"I know, I know—you can't give out personal information. But you can't blame a guy for trying. Good night, Operator 322. Maybe I'll see you around."

"Good night, Sir," I said, ending the call.

I'd had flirty callers before, but this one was different. He was the only one who ever called back—and the details he gave about himself, his unusual last name, where he worked, that story about being new in town—they were oddly specific.

I wouldn't say I was interested, exactly. More intrigued by this Ramon Dormido, if that was really his name.

A former classmate of mine, Lila, had a boyfriend, Antonio, who worked for Philippine Airlines. Maybe he'd know this Ramon.

We met for lunch one day, and I told them about the strange caller.

"Oh yeah, I know him," Antonio said. "That's Ramon—Ramon Dormido. He's the new guy, just came in from Negros. Good-looking fellow, and single, if you're interested."

"Uh, no, of course I'm not interested. Just curious, that's all. His last name is unusual—it means 'asleep' in Spanish. I thought he was pulling some kind of prank."

The look on their faces told me they didn't know what *Dormido* meant.

"Well, anyway, thanks," I said. "At least now I know he's a real person."

I didn't know it then, but the next day, Antonio saw Ramon at work and told him about our odd little conversation.

"Hey, Ramon! Your new friend was asking about you."

"What are you talking about?" Ramon asked, puzzled.

"Your new friend, Ging Ramon, the pretty mestiza phone operator at PLDT. She and my girlfriend went to school together."

It immediately clicked with Ramon. And more importantly, he now knew my name.

On my next shift, I received another direct call.

"Operator 322, how may I help you?"

"Why hello, Operator 322. How are you doing this evening? Or should I call you *Ging*? Which would you prefer?"

I could almost hear him smirking on the other end.

"Sir," I began.

"Please—call me Ramon. I think we can dispense with the formalities now that we know each other's names."

"Sir," I said firmly, "we aren't allowed to conduct personal calls while at work. I could get in trouble."

"Is your supervisor there?"

"No, but—"

"Then nobody will know. You won't get in trouble."

He had a point. The supervisor wasn't there, and it was a slow night. I didn't want to sound too eager, but truthfully, I was curious about this mysterious man from Negros.

"Tell you what," he said. "You're probably shy and don't want to say too much about yourself. So why don't you ask me questions—anything you want."

My interest was piqued. His playful flirting was beginning to disarm me.

"Okay," I said, smiling to myself. "So, what do you look like?"

"Oh, well, sorry to tell you—I have the face of a monkey. The kind of face only a mother could love. That's one of the reasons I had to leave Negros. Nobody wanted to be friends with me."

I couldn't help but laugh.

"I'm sure that's not true."

"There's only one way to find out," he replied. "Meet me for ice cream, and you'll get to see the talking monkey for yourself."

I laughed again. "I don't know…"

"There's a café near the telephone office—you know the one?"

"Yes, I know it."

"Meet me there tomorrow at 12:30 p.m., if you'd like to get to know me better. If you don't show up, I'll get the message. And I promise, I won't bother you again."

I didn't know what to say.

"Have a good evening, Miss Ramon. I hope I see you tomorrow."

After the call ended, my heart pounded, trying to process the absurdity of it all. This man—this voice I'd been speaking to—no longer felt like an anonymous stranger. I was more than intrigued; I genuinely wanted to meet him.

That night, I couldn't stop thinking about his offer. Part of me wanted to keep the mystery alive, to stay safely behind the wire and the anonymity of my switchboard. But another part—maybe the braver part—wanted to step beyond it. To see if the connection I felt over the phone was as real in person as it seemed through the lines.

By morning, I'd made up my mind. I was going to meet Ramon for ice cream.

41 Love And Porridge

I wasn't sure what to expect when I went to meet Ramon that afternoon. I remember thinking, *Was this a mistake?* After Orlando and Tomas, was I rushing into things again? But when he walked through the door, the second-guessing stopped. I hadn't known what he looked like, yet somehow I recognized him instantly. There was something familiar in his smile, as if we'd already met somewhere before. He wasn't quite what I expected, but he was handsome. Almost as soon as he sat down, we began talking like old friends. Over melting ice cream, we traded stories about our families, sharing small pieces of our lives. The hours slipped by, and before we knew it, it was time to go. After that day, he started meeting me after work, waiting outside the telephone office to walk me home.

Our walks home soon became a routine, though at times our conflicting schedules made it difficult for him to join me. When he could, he insisted on walking me the whole way, his presence a comforting balm after a long day.

As we walked, I learned more about Ramon and his dreams. Although he worked as a radio technician at Philippine Airlines, he longed to become a pilot. He spoke of airplanes, the thrill of takeoffs, and the distant places they flew. I listened, enraptured, as he painted vivid pictures of lands far from our own.

"I want to explore, to see the world beyond the Philippines," he said, his eyes glinting with hope. I found myself captivated, eager to glimpse the world through his adventurous spirit.

"And one day, I'll make it to America!"

"Do you really think you will?" I asked.

"Well, you know what they say—where there's a will, there's a way!"

His dreams felt so distant, so wildly ambitious—so unlike Orlando, who had always seemed content to stay grounded. Yet there was something in Ramon's voice, a quiet certainty, that made me believe he just might succeed.

One day, he surprised me by inviting me to lunch at his favorite diner—a little hole-in-the-wall restaurant tucked away in a narrow alley, known for its *lugaw*, a comforting rice porridge. It was a change from our usual routine, and though I hesitated, something in his earnest eyes made me say yes.

As we stepped into the modest eatery, the rich aroma of simmering broth wrapped around us like a warm embrace. Ramon's eyes lit up, and I couldn't help but smile at his enthusiasm.

"This is the best lugaw in the city!" he declared, practically bouncing on his toes. "They simmer the chicken for hours to make the broth—so rich and full of flavor!"

We settled into a small wooden table, and I watched as he ordered, his animated gestures punctuating his words. He spoke with the same excitement as he described the toppings—crisp toasted garlic, fresh green onions, salted soybeans for a savory kick, and boiled eggs to make the dish heartier.

When our bowls finally arrived, steaming and fragrant, I couldn't help but admire how he relished each moment. "Just look at that broth!" he said, his eyes wide with delight as he lifted his spoon to his lips. He slurped it up with gusto, a look of pure bliss on his face. It was endearing to watch, and I found myself laughing at the sheer joy he took in something so simple.

He noticed my amusement and grinned, his cheeks flushing slightly. "What? It's delicious! You have to try it." He gestured for me to take a spoonful, and I obliged—the warm, velvety texture filling my mouth. It was just as comforting as he had promised, a hug in a bowl.

"I can't believe I've never eaten here before," I admitted, savoring the flavors.

"I told you!" he beamed, looking so proud, like a child showing off his favorite toy. "You see, this is the kind of thing that makes life worthwhile—simple pleasures, you know?"

As we dug into our bowls, the conversation flowed as easily as ever. Between bites of savory lugaw, we caught up on our week and laughed over little things that had happened at work. Then, his tone shifted.

"Ging," he began, a hint of excitement in his voice, "I have some important news to share."

I leaned in, my curiosity piqued. "What is it?"

"The US Navy is accepting applicants for an exam to enlist," he announced. "It's a pathway to America—and citizenship."

My heart skipped a beat. I could see the dream of a new life flickering in his eyes, the thrill of adventure dancing across his face.

"That's amazing, Ramon!" I said, genuinely happy for him. "You've talked about going to America since we met. This is a big step!"

But then the implication sank in. What would this mean for us? Would his dream take him away for good? The questions churned quietly inside me, even as I smiled. Ramon must have sensed my hesitation, because he leaned closer, looking intently into my eyes.

"The exam's still several weeks away," he assured me. "I have a lot of studying to do, so I'm not going anywhere soon."

"I'm excited for you," I said, hoping to ease the doubts brewing in my heart. "You're smart, Ramon. You'll do well on the exam."

His face lit up, hope sparking anew. "Thanks, Ging. It means a lot to have your support. I really believe this could be my chance."

He went back to his bowl, and I followed suit, savoring the warmth and comfort of the meal. But the excitement of our lunch had shifted, taking on a bittersweet note.

"I'm glad we're having this lunch," he said softly, cutting through my thoughts. "It feels like everything's falling into place."

I nodded, my heart swelling with pride for him—even as a small part of me began to brace for the distance that might come.

He paused, thoughtful, then reached across the table and took my hand. "Whatever happens, I want you to know—you're part of this journey for me. I don't want to lose you."

A rush of warmth flooded through me at his words, a wave of reassurance that brought a smile to my lips. "You won't lose me, Ramon. Whatever it takes to pursue your dreams, I'll be cheering you on every step of the way."

As he squeezed my hand, I felt hopeful. Perhaps this wasn't an ending but a beginning—a chance for both of us to grow. The idea of America seemed daunting yet thrilling, a world where his aspirations might unfold. Would I be part of that world? I didn't know. But with each spoonful of lugaw, I let go of my worries, embracing the possibilities ahead—hopeful our paths would still converge in ways we couldn't yet imagine.

42 The Promise

Over the next several weeks, Ramon and I tried to make the most of our time together. As confident as he was, neither of us knew if he would pass the exam—or how long we'd have before he'd have to ship off for boot camp. On our days off and in between his study sessions, we went on picnics, watched movies, or simply spent time with each other.

By this time, Ramon was well acquainted with most of my family and friends. I introduced him to Dolly and Lourdes early on. Ramon was a great dancer and soon became part of our group. Papa Emilio even met him during one of his business trips. Unlike Orlando, he was genuinely impressed.

"I like him, Ging. He's smart and ambitious! And he's going to join the US Navy and go to America; he's definitely going places!" he said excitedly.

"Papa, it's not certain yet. He hasn't even taken the exam."

"Well, whatever. He's still better than that boring one—what was his name?"

"Orlando," I replied.

"Yes, Orlando. That guy… *es muy aburrido*."

"Papa!" I protested, trying not to laugh.

"Now Ramon, he is exciting! And comes from a good family too. Didn't you say he has two brothers who are priests and a sister who's a nun? He's a good man to marry."

I was thrilled that Papa Emilio approved of Ramon. But I reminded myself he hadn't even proposed yet.

The day before the exam, I could tell Ramon was nervous. We didn't stay out late, so he would be well-rested. Before he left, I gave him a hug, kissed him on the cheek, and wished him good luck.

The next day was nerve-racking. I moved through my shift in a daze, my hands working the switchboard while my thoughts stayed with Ramon. When I met him later and asked how he had done, he replied he didn't know.

"I think I did okay," he said. "It was a tough exam, and I knew a lot of the answers. I guess we'll just have to wait and see."

About a month later, Ramon was waiting for me after my shift. The big smile on his face told me all I needed to know.

"I passed the exam!" he exclaimed. "I've been accepted into the US Navy."

As he pulled me into a big hug, the weight of it slowly sank in. I felt proud and happy for him, but I couldn't entirely shake a heaviness in my chest. Ramon had spoken of America often enough, his far-off look appearing whenever he mentioned new places and big dreams. A part of me had thought they were just dreams. Now here he was, one step closer to achieving them.

Stepping back from our embrace, he looked at me, eyes gleaming with excitement.

"This is my big chance, Ging! To go to America, to become a US citizen. I'll be able to send money back, help my family here. It's... everything I've dreamed of."

I asked the question I had been dreading.

"When do you leave?"

"In three weeks. That's when I ship off for San Diego, California, for boot camp."

I was slightly stunned. Three weeks felt impossibly close.

He saw the disappointment and sadness on my face. Reaching for my hands, their warmth steady against mine, he said softly:

"You know this is something I have to do. But I want you to wait for me."

He hesitated, lines of his face softening, eyes meeting mine with a newfound vulnerability.

"When I come back, I'll marry you. I want you to be my wife."

For a moment, my heart soared. But a small voice whispered that he had never once told me he loved me. In all these months together, sharing bits of our lives, he had never said the words. Could I wait faithfully, with no promises other than his offer of marriage? I squeezed his hands, searching his face for confirmation that he felt as deeply as I did. But all I saw was the excitement of his dream, his journey to America.

The morning of his departure arrived far too quickly, the city muted as if holding its breath. The ferry terminal was crowded, bustling with people wrapped in their own stories of reunion and goodbye. I spotted Ramon near the edge of the pier, duffel bag slung over his shoulder, eyes scanning the crowd until they landed on me. He broke into a smile, and my worries quieted.

As I reached him, he took my hands in his, holding them tightly.

"Ging," he said softly. "Thank you for coming to see me off. I know it's a lot to ask, but please—don't forget me. I'll think of you every day."

I swallowed hard and smiled through the tremor in my voice.

"Don't worry, Ramon. I'll keep you in my prayers."

He pulled me into a tight embrace, strong arms holding me as though trying to imprint the memory of us into his bones. Then, as we parted, he leaned in for a gentle, tender kiss, leaving me breathless.

"I love you, Ging," he whispered, barely more than a breath. "I'll come back for you."

Every shadow of doubt vanished. Those words, finally spoken, were all I needed.

"I'll wait for you, Ramon," I said, my voice steady and full of promise.

He held my gaze a moment longer, eyes soft, before releasing my hands. I watched as he stepped onto the ferry, turning to wave one last time before disappearing into the crowd. As the ferry pulled away, carrying him to Manila, to America, to the life he had dreamed of, a strange certainty settled within me. Somehow, I knew he would keep his promise—and I would be waiting.

43 Crossroad

My brother-in-law Felix was deeply protective of his sisters-in-law, caring for us as if we were his own sisters. He had always wanted more for us, and for him, that meant seeking a life in America. Like many Filipinos of that generation, Felix admired Americans, grateful for the sacrifices made by the US military during the war. He loved befriending the Americans he met, usually soldiers and sailors stationed on the islands. His job at the movie theater gave him plenty of opportunities, as off-duty military personnel often came to catch a bit of home in American films. One of these soldiers was a man named Bill.

"Ging, you should meet him," Felix said, looking up from his lunch of stewed fish and rice. His words were equal parts invitation and command.

I wiped my hands on my apron and glanced at Helen, who was busy mending a torn hem. She didn't raise an eyebrow. This was typical of Felix—always imagining our futures, ones he believed shouldn't be confined to the Philippines.

"Him?" I asked, trying to sound casual, though I knew exactly who he meant.

"An American soldier," he confirmed, looking me in the eye. "A good man. He's stationed here in Cebu for now, but soon he'll return to the States."

Helen sighed softly, the way she did whenever Felix talked about Americans. She understood his intentions. Since their marriage, he had been determined to see his sisters-in-law matched with GIs—men who could offer more than the Philippines could provide. For him, it wasn't just about love; it was about opportunity.

Unlike Felix, I didn't dream of going to America, nor did I see it as the key to a better life. I had a good job, earned a decent paycheck, and felt I could build a full life here in the Philippines without leaving home.

"You should think about it," he pressed. "Your life could be different. Better. The Americans, they live well—and they take care of their wives."

"But what about you?" I countered. "Don't you take good care of Helen?"

"I'm the exception," he chuckled, winking at her.

I bit my lip and looked out the window at the gentle sway of the nearby coconut trees. I thought of Ramon at boot camp, remembering the letters he sent several times a week—each filled with love, longing, and the promise of our future together. He wanted to marry me, and I had promised I'd wait for him.

"But what about Ramon? He wants to marry me," I said quietly.

Felix and Helen had been urging me to move on for months. Their words were persistent, yet caring, like a steady tide pressing at the edges of my resolve.

"He's not coming back for you," they'd insist. "He'll find an American girl and forget you."

"You're young, beautiful, and single. See what else is out there. Besides, he didn't even give you an engagement ring—so you're not officially engaged."

Their words stung. There was truth in them I couldn't ignore. We weren't officially engaged—no ring, no formal promise—just the dream of a young man in a distant country and the future we'd imagined together. While I wanted to hold onto that dream, a part of me wavered. Maybe it was time to confront reality and consider other paths.

Felix stood, dabbing his mouth with a napkin, his eyes steady. "He's coming over tomorrow," he said, as if the decision had already been made. "Just meet him. That's all I'm asking."

I nodded, though a knot had already formed in my stomach.

The next day came too soon. The house was filled with the smell of freshly cooked adobo, and I busied myself in the kitchen, trying to keep my hands from shaking.

Helen helped me pick out the dress I wore—a yellow gingham halter-neck, cinched just right at the waist and flaring out like a sunbeam caught in motion.

"You look beautiful," she whispered, squeezing my hand. I knew she meant it, but there was something in her voice that sounded sad. Helen had always supported Felix's plans, but I wondered if she, too, felt the weight of what he was asking of me.

When the knock finally came, my heart skipped a beat. I straightened my dress and stepped into the living room, where Felix was already greeting the guest.

"Ging, this is Bill," Felix said, his voice unusually bright.

The man beside him was tall, his skin pale and lightly freckled under the afternoon sun. His dark hair was neatly trimmed, and his glasses framed a pair of clear blue eyes. He smiled broadly and extended his hand. I took it, my own trembling slightly.

"Nice to meet you," he said, radiating an earnest warmth. I smiled, though I barely found the courage to say much in return.

For the next hour, we sat and talked—though most of the conversation flowed between Felix and Bill. Felix was at ease, chatting about the postwar years, life in the Philippines for US servicemen, and the opportunities waiting in America. Bill nodded often, smiling, occasionally glancing at me as if to gauge my reaction. I could feel his eyes on me, but I was too shy to meet them directly.

As the sun began to set, Bill stood to leave, thanking us for our hospitality. Felix walked him to the door, exchanging a few quiet words I couldn't hear. When he returned, he smiled softly.

"Well?" he asked.

"He seems nice," I answered.

"Is that it? He seems nice?"

"Felix," I said, half-smiling, "what did you expect? That I'd marry the first American you brought to our house?"

He chuckled, shaking his head. "Okay, I get it. But at least try to get to know him better."

I sighed, feeling the weight of his hope pressing on me. Bill had been kind, polite, even a little charming. But my heart wasn't ready to leap toward something new, not while another promise still lingered in the corners of my mind.

Felix placed a hand on my shoulder and gave it a gentle squeeze. He wasn't one to press too hard, but I knew what he wanted—for me to see beyond what he thought was our simple life in Cebu. He wanted me to dream bigger, to imagine a future beyond the islands.

I nodded, not wanting to disappoint him, though inside, I was still skeptical that marrying an American was what was best for me.

In the weeks that followed, Bill continued to visit. Each time, he brought with him a warmth that seeped quietly into the corners of my heart. He'd arrive with a smile that lit up his freckled face, eager to share stories about his life in Wisconsin—tales of snow-covered fields, summer fairs, and the wildflowers that painted the countryside. Our conversations flowed more easily, and as I learned about his world, I found myself drawn to him in ways I hadn't expected.

After each visit, I couldn't help feeling a pang of guilt. Even though we were only friends, it felt like a quiet betrayal of Ramon. His letters, once arriving almost daily, had begun to taper off. The long, affectionate pages gave way to short, matter-of-fact notes. Maybe what everyone said was true—maybe Ramon had moved on.

One evening, as we sat out front watching the sun fade into the horizon, Bill took my hand. "I've written my mother about you," he said, his voice steady but full of warmth. "She wants to know everything—what you like, what you dream about, how you feel."

My heart raced. "What did you tell her?" I asked, half-joking, though genuinely curious.

"I told her you're the most beautiful woman I've ever met," he said, smiling. "And that I've fallen head over heels in love with you."

Before I could respond, he reached into his pocket and pulled out a folded letter. "She sent this for you. I hope that's alright."

I took the letter, my hands trembling slightly as I unfolded the crisp pages. Bill watched me closely, his blue eyes filled with anticipation.

Dear Ging,

I hope this letter finds you well. I've heard so much about you from Bill, and I want you to know how happy he is to have met you. I can see how much he cares for you, and as his mother, that means the world to me. I dream of the day when I can call you my daughter-in-law, and I want you to know that you would be a wonderful addition to our family.

Life here in Wisconsin is different from what you know, but I believe you would love it. Bill speaks of your kindness and beauty, and I can tell he has fallen for you deeply. You have captured his heart, and I pray that you might feel the same.

With all my love,

Mrs. Payton

Tears blurred my vision as I read. The kindness of this woman I had never met enveloped me, each line glowing with warmth and hope. Bill had written home about me—and his mother was reaching out, welcoming me into a life that felt like a dream.

When I looked up, Bill was smiling softly, pride and longing mingling in his expression.

"She means every word, Ging. I've never felt like this about anyone before. You make me feel alive. I want to marry you."

"But we haven't even known each other that long," I said, my heart aching with uncertainty. "What if I'm not who you think I am?"

He squeezed my hand gently. "You are everything I hoped for and more. I know marrying me and moving to America might seem daunting, but I can't imagine a future without you."

"But what about Ramon?" I asked quietly. "He asked me to marry him too. And I told him I would wait."

Bill nodded, his voice calm but his eyes heavy. "I know you love Ramon, and I respect that. But you can't wait forever."

"I need time to think," I said finally, my voice barely above a whisper.

"I understand," he replied. "Take all the time you need. I'll be here."

In the weeks that followed, my feelings grew more tangled. Bill and I continued to see each other, and my heart—still bound to Ramon—was slowly drifting elsewhere. Ramon's letters had nearly stopped, and each passing day made me question whether waiting still made sense.

Then one day, a letter arrived—the letter that changed everything.

It was from Ramon. He apologized for not writing and for the brevity of his letters. He explained that he'd been deployed on a ship where mail service was infrequent, and that they were forbidden from writing much detail for security reasons. But he had good news: he would be returning to the Philippines soon. He couldn't say when, but he intended to marry me when he got back.

He was keeping his promise. Ramon was coming back to me.

As I stood outside our house, rereading his letter, Bill appeared at the gate. I looked up, and our eyes met. From my expression alone, he seemed to understand.

"Good news?" he asked quietly.

"It's from Ramon," I said, almost a whisper. "He'll be coming back soon."

Bill nodded, his voice soft but sincere. "That's wonderful, Ging. I'm really happy for you."

He had a box of candy in his hands.

"I brought these for you," he said, offering them awkwardly.

"Thank you," I smiled. "Why don't you come inside? I'll get you something cold to drink."

He shook his head. "I should be getting back to base."

Bill stepped closer and hugged me. I can still remember the scent of his cologne, the warmth of his embrace—the quiet ache of goodbye.

"I wish you the best, Ging," he whispered in my ear.

Then he turned and walked down the street. We never saw each other again after that.

I stood there, flooded by emotions I could barely name. The joy of knowing Ramon was coming back, and the sorrow of losing a man who might have been my future.

That evening, I thought about Ramon—about our plans, our life together in America, maybe even beyond. But I also thought about Bill, and the life I might have had with him. I thought of Wisconsin, a place I could barely imagine but which Bill had brought to life through his stories. I thought of his mother, a woman I had never met, welcoming me with open arms.

As Ramon's return drew near, I pushed thoughts of Bill aside and focused on what was ahead.

Many years later, after a lifetime of watching children and grandchildren grow up, I came across a picture of Bill tucked between the pages of an old album. I paused, holding it in my hands, and thought of what could have been. I pictured him in his beloved Wisconsin—walking across a snowy field, standing among wildflowers, or gazing at the stars on one of those clear nights from his backyard. Perhaps looking up at the same stars I could see from mine.

And maybe, just maybe, he was thinking of me too.

44 A Bright Future

I arrived in Negros a few days before Ramon's ship was scheduled to dock in Manila. With the wedding fast approaching, there was so much to prepare and so little time.

Ramon had put me in touch with his sisters and cousins, who would help arrange the ceremony and reception, ensuring everything was ready for our big day.

For the next few days, the house was alive with activity. The townspeople were busy preparing too. Our wedding date coincided with a local fiesta. In the town square, people strung colorful *banderitas* across the streets and set up stalls promising a feast of *lechon*, *lumpia*, and *kakanin*. The air buzzed with anticipation. I knew the excitement wasn't just for me and Ramon, but at times it felt as though it was.

Father Manuel, Ramon's older brother, was a soft-spoken man whose serene presence seemed to command respect effortlessly. When he met me for the first time, his voice was gentle yet firm.

"Ging, it is a joy to welcome you into our family. Ramon is a fortunate man."

The next day, he took me to the church—St. Joseph—where we would be married. The beautiful old stone structure stood proudly at the center of town. Inside, its high ceilings and stained glass windows filled the space with a warm, golden light. The altar, adorned with flowers and candles, radiated a quiet sanctity.

Father Manuel shared his plans for the celebration.

"This year's fiesta is particularly special," he said. "It coincides with my birthday. What better gift could I receive than the chance to officiate Ramon's wedding?"

I smiled, thinking how lucky we were to celebrate our union with both family and the town he spoke so lovingly of.

As the days passed, I felt drawn into the rhythm of Ramon's family and their town. Yet each moment of joy carried a bittersweet ache of longing. My thoughts drifted to Ramon. What would it feel like to see him again after so long? Would he have changed? Would I? I counted the hours until his arrival, imagining the sound of his voice, the feel of his arms around me, the moment we would finally stand together as husband and wife.

The night before Ramon's arrival, I stood by my window, staring out at the moonlit fields. Fiesta music floated in the distance. I thought about Mama Caring and Papa Peping, who wouldn't be able to attend. Ramon's return had come so suddenly, there was no time to arrange for them to travel. It saddened me that they could not be there, but I was glad that Mama Doray, Carlota, and Jun would be present to celebrate this new chapter in my life.

I closed my eyes and whispered a prayer—not just for the wedding, but for the love that had carried us through years and across oceans. Soon, he would be here, and the waiting would be over.

The morning of our wedding, the church bells rang out in joyous peals, echoing over the bustling town of Saravia. Inside the centuries-old church, sunlight poured through the stained glass windows, painting the aisle in hues of gold, blue, and red. The air smelled of fresh flowers and incense, mingling with the soft murmur of voices from our guests.

I stood at the entrance, heart pounding, one hand clutching my bouquet of sampaguita and orchids, the other resting gently on the arm of my nephew, Jun. At seventeen, he carried himself with an earnestness far beyond his years. He insisted on wearing his best *barong tagalog*, and though it was a little large, he looked proud and determined.

As the first chords of the wedding march swelled from the organ, Jun turned to me with wide, tear-filled eyes.

"Tita Ging," he whispered, his voice cracking, "Papa Emilio would be so happy for you."

A lump formed in my throat. I could almost see Papa Emilio standing beside me, his hands steady, his eyes carrying that quiet warmth. He had passed away earlier that year, and though time had softened the pain, the ache of his absence remained.

I blinked back tears and placed a hand on Jun's cheek. He nodded, his face crumpling briefly before he steadied himself. Together, we began the walk down the aisle.

Ramon stood at the altar, resplendent in his US Navy service dress blue uniform—the familiar "crackerjack" sailor attire. I remember how handsome and dashing he looked, his dark eyes fixed on me with an intensity that made the entire church seem to blur. I barely noticed the gathered crowd; all I saw was him.

When we reached the altar, Jun let go of my arm, hesitating only for a moment before hugging me tightly.

"I'm so happy for you, Tita," he whispered. I kissed his forehead, and Father Manuel smiled before beginning the ceremony.

Our vows were simple yet sacred, spoken in both English and *Hiligaynon*, the prominent dialect of Negros. When Father Manuel pronounced us husband and wife, the church erupted into applause. Ramon's hands were steady as he lifted my veil and kissed me—warm and sure—as if sealing every promise we had ever made.

By the time we reached the town square, the celebration was in full swing. A parade of dancers and drummers welcomed us. Tables overflowed with *lechon*, *kare-kare*, *kaldereta*, *pancit*, and rice. People of all ages mingled and laughed, swept up in the festive music. Ramon and I joined in the dances, hands clasped, moving to the lively beat of traditional folk songs.

Yet amidst the joy, I glanced skyward, imagining Papa Emilio watching over us. I whispered a silent prayer of gratitude, hoping he could feel the happiness radiating from this day.

As dusk fell, the town square glowed with lanterns and fireflies. The celebration stretched into the night. Later, as the crowds thinned, Ramon and I made our rounds, thanking family and friends for sharing in this momentous occasion. Afterwards, we retreated to the second floor of his brother's house, our first night alone as husband and wife.

With his arm around me and my head resting on his shoulder, we stood by the window, gazing out at the fading fiesta below. The faint glow of lanterns dotted the streets, and laughter softened as families retired for the night. Outside, the last bursts of firecrackers lit the sky—a perfect reflection of the fireworks in my heart. It was the happiest day of my life.

As we stood there, the world outside growing quiet, a deep, unshakable peace settled over me. Ramon was here. We were together. And for the first time in years, the future felt as bright as the stars above, promising everything we had hoped for and more.

Epilogue

Sitting by the window, watching the sun dip below the horizon, I find myself reflecting on a life that has been, in every sense, full and extraordinary. My journey began in the shadow of war, growing up during the Japanese occupation of the Philippines in World War II. Those were dark times, marked by fear and uncertainty, but also by the unbreakable bond of family. Together, we faced hunger, loss, and the daily struggle for survival—and together, we endured. We were living proof that, even in the harshest conditions, love and resilience could prevail.

As a young woman, I imagined my life unfolding with fairy-tale simplicity. I envisioned meeting my Prince Charming, and together we would overcome life's challenges—like battling imaginary dragons—and live happily ever after. However, life had other plans. The man I married was not the one I had dreamed of. He struggled with his own demons—alcoholism and gambling—and the road we traveled together was anything but smooth. Yet, from that union came my greatest treasures: our six children, each a unique and beautiful gift. Raising them was no easy task, especially amidst the struggles in our marriage, but it remains the most rewarding chapter of my life.

When I was a teenager, a carnival fortune teller peered into my palm and spoke of distant places I would one day visit. At the time, I laughed, dismissing it as mere fantasy. Yet, life has a way of surprising us. Over the years, I have gazed at the serene temples of Japan, walked the cobblestone streets of Europe, marveled at the monuments in our nation's capital, and dipped my feet in the Sea of Galilee. Each journey, big or small, felt like a step closer to fulfilling that long-ago prophecy.

Now, as I look back, I see a tapestry woven with threads of joy and sorrow, triumph and trial. But I choose to dwell not on the hardships but on the blessings that have graced my life. I see the love of family that carried me through the war. I see the faces of my children, grandchildren, and great grandchildren, each a testament to hope and endurance. I see the sunsets from every corner of the world, reminding me of life's fleeting beauty and its infinite grace.

Life has not been perfect, but it has been mine—full of lessons, growth, and above all, love. And as the sun sets on this chapter, I rest in the comfort of gratitude, knowing I have truly lived.

A Life Lived

The main story closes on a note of hope in the mid-1950s. The accompanying images, spanning the past several decades, are a tribute to the family and prosperity that followed the struggle, proving that the spirit of resilience, like love, endures.

Photo with an unnamed American soldier and Carlota's children: Jun, Mits, Jenny, and Carlito. Notice they look noticeably thinner than I do.

My brother Ricardo, the soldier who visited me after the liberation.

"Mickey Mouse" money issued by the Japanese during the occupation. (Image courtesy of Utah State University Special Collections)

CABALLES MELITON	CPL	57 INF REGT (PS)	PHILIPPINES
CABALQUINTO SIXTO C	PVT	45 INF REGT (PS)	PHILIPPINES
CABALUNO MAXIMO	CPL	HQ CO PHIL DEPT	PHILIPPINES
CABANA MIGUEL A	PVT	57 INF REGT (PS)	PHILIPPINES
CABANATAN JUAN	PVT	57 INF REGT (PS)	PHILIPPINES
CABANATUAN IGNACIO	PFC	92 CA REGT (PS)	PHILIPPINES
CABANCE SILVINO	PFC	86 FA BN (PS)	PHILIPPINES
CABANDO ENRIQUE	PFC	45 INF REGT (PS)	PHILIPPINES
CABANDO FORTUNATO	PVT	2 GEN HOSP	PHILIPPINES
CABANES SABAS	PVT	QM CORPS (PS)	PHILIPPINES
CABANEZ JESUS A	TEC 5	12 MED BN (PS)	PHILIPPINES
CABANGISAN AGAPITO	PVT	57 INF REGT (PS)	PHILIPPINES

Inscription on the Walls of the Missing at the Manila American Cemetery for my uncle, Corporal Meliton Caballes.

The Book of Ging

Photo Mama Doray had taken of me shortly after the war ended.

School photo from Zapatera Elementary in Cebu.

Here I am holding my pet civet (*musang* in Tagalog). Joseling gave it to me after the war. Although some people still keep them as pets, civets are now known for a special coffee produced by harvesting partially digested coffee cherries, which the animals have eaten and defecated.

Visiting a cemetery with classmates during All Souls' Day.

With my dance troupe from the University of San Carlos.

Graduation day at the University of San Carlos.

My sister Penang and I with our Mama Caring.

Penang and I with Julio before going to a dance.

Ramon and I during a beach outing, while we were still dating.

Ramon shortly after his arrival in Cebu.

A photo taken of me at the beach, sent to Ramon while he was at boot camp.

Ramon was fascinated with aviation. He was a radio technician with Philippine Airlines but dreamed of becoming a pilot.

Ramon visiting Knott's Berry Farm on shore leave after boot camp.

Ramon posing on Waikiki Beach during liberty on Oahu.

Ramon's first car, purchased after he was stationed in the Philippines.

Our wedding photo.

Photo with our first child, Irene.

Ramon and Irene at her first birthday party.

Mama Doray and I at her home in Manila.

My Papa Peping.

This photo with my siblings, Mama Caring, and aunt was taken after Papa Peping's funeral.

Front row (from left): Benjie, Pina. Middle row (from left): Nora (Nene's wife), Penang, Ging, Mama Caring, Tia Tilde, Nena, Helen. Back row (from left): Julie, Diegs (Julie's husband), Nene, Julio, Salvador, Nene (Salvador's wife).

Family portrait photo taken in Japan, circa 1963:
Back row: Ging and Ramon.
Front row (from left): Ramon, Ruth, Reuben, and Irene.

Ramon's promotion to Petty Officer First Class (E-6).

Visiting Nagasaki, with the port visible in the background.

Photo taken at Naval Air Station Alameda in 1966, a few months after we arrived in the US: I am holding Richard, the newest addition to our family. Standing behind the kids is Jun (Carlota's son).

Photo with the kids, Christmas 1971.

Portrait photo taken after Ramon's retirement from the US Navy.

Visiting the Eiffel Tower during my first trip to Europe, June 1984.

One of my many visits to Disneyland.

Portrait photo taken for our 40th wedding anniversary.

Irene and I at the Palace of Versailles on my fourth trip to Europe.

Visiting the Pearl Harbor National Memorial on Oahu.

Dipping my feet in the Sea of Galilee.

Exploring Petra, Jordan.

My oldest son, Reuben, who passed away at age 33. I think of him every day.

My children—my greatest accomplishment and greatest treasures in life.

Front row (from left): Ruth, Ging, Irene. Back row (from left): Ron, Richard, Ramon.

What's In A Name?

Spanish colonial rule left an indelible mark on the Philippines. It shaped our faith, our language, our towns—and the very names our families still carry. Ours, too, comes from that time: a trace of history that found its way into our story, passed quietly from one generation to the next.

According to family legend, my husband Ramon's great-great-grandfather was a tax collector for the Spanish government. For a Filipino, it was a despised job—taking money from your countrymen to enrich the coffers of the colonizers.

The daily pressures of the job eventually took their toll. Instead of carrying out his duties, he began taking long naps each day. Eventually, his Spanish overseers noticed that revenue from his province was falling behind and set out to investigate. They were shocked and deeply upset to find their Filipino tax collector sleeping under a tree.

As punishment, he was demoted, and his family's surname was changed from *Claridad*—which means "clear" or "clarity"—to *Dormido*, literally meaning "asleep" in Spanish.

And that is the origin of the name we carry: a legacy of colonial rule, quiet rebellion, and a good long nap.

About The Authors

Ging Dormido is a survivor of the WWII occupation of the Philippines. The wife of a US Navy veteran, she and her husband established roots in California, where they raised six children. Ging is a self-proclaimed 'Jill of all trades,' having worked as a telephone operator, cannery worker, waitress, bank teller, and payroll specialist, among other jobs. She currently lives in the San Francisco Bay Area.

Ron Dormido, the fifth child of Ging, is a retired US Army veteran. After years of talking about his post-retirement plans to take up surfing and learn the ukulele, he instead undertook this project to preserve his mother's extraordinary story for future generations.

Ging and Ron at Matsumoto's Shave Ice on the North Shore of Oahu.

Made in the USA
Coppell, TX
26 February 2026

72451217R00135